SING!

SING!

Business and Life Lessons
from the Karaoke Stage

by

Steve "Doc" Dragoo

Music expresses that which cannot be put into words and that which cannot remain silent.

—Victor Hugo[i]

Table of Contents

Foreword

As my partner Jim Gilmore and I like to stress, goods and services are no longer enough. What people want today are experiences—memorable events that engage them in an inherently personal way. That's why so many companies are getting into the business of experience staging. Think of the rise of theme parks, theme restaurants, experiential retail, boutique hotels, cafes...

And karaoke. While it originated as a fad in the 1970s, karaoke did not explode into pop cultural consciousness until the 1990s. It's no coincidence that during that same decade we saw the "Experience Economy" explode into the business management consciousness.

Only one person stands at the forefront of both the "Experience Economy" and Karaoke—Steve Dragoo. In a decade of knowing Steve, I've discovered he's an astute consultant, a food expert, and a singer (not to mention one of the nicest gentleman you will ever meet.) But perhaps most importantly he's the only person in the world who is both a CE and KJ! Meaning, Steve is one of our over 200 Certified Experts in the "Experience Economy" around the world and the only one who has performed as a Karaoke Jockey.

In fact, Steve's not only a CE, but he's also the very first one, the Certified "Experience Economy" Expert #001. When we first announced the program in 2006 he submitted his application immediately, and just as immediately Jim and I approved it. And no one since has embodied the mantle of being a CE more so than Steve. He has not only read *The Experience Economy* book over ten times but he has also worked tirelessly over the past decade to enhance the experiences of grocery stores, charcuteries, and countless other businesses. He even developed his own workbook on the "Experience Economy" to train frontline workers to engage each and every guest.

In fact, Steve is not just a karaoke enthusiast and occasional KJ but he's also the one and only Dr. Groove, the character he takes on whenever he gets in a karaoke venue to personally live out the "Experience Economy" for his audiences. He strives tirelessly to not only create a great experience for everyone in the place, but in particular focuses on helping every singer up there, bringing out their best and making them the star of the show.

One of the principles Steve internalized in all his years studying the "Experience Economy" and that he personally exemplifies as Dr. Groove is that work IS theatre. It's not a metaphor (work as theatre) but a model. Whenever people are in front of customers they are on stage; whether they know it or not, whether they do it well or not, they are on stage and need to act in a way that engages the audience. So just as every karaoke song is performed on a literal stage, so too does every person perform on the business stage.

And it is that exact connection between stage performance and business performance that Steve mines so well in this wonderful book. Just as Dr. Groove brings out the best in the karaoke singers he supports, Steve Dragoo (I think I'm going to start calling him Steve DRaGroove from now on...) will bring out the best in every reader. He will inspire you to fulfill Steve's groovy slogan—Step up, Inspire and be Inspired, Find Your Nexus, and Go For It—to make your own business performances SING.

That being said, Steve has organized this book in bite-size chunks that can be comsumed and read, almost like afeast— with entrées to be digested, pondered, and used for energy, or to be picked up any time as starters to nibble on and inspire. Each section begins with the same initial as the four main chapters, and believe me you could get a heckuva lot out of this book just by reading the headers! They speak volumes, or rather sing melodies, but the text itself backs up these usually-one-word soliloquys with a page or two of sonnets. They will help you Step Up, Inspire you to greatness, find your Nexus, and Go forward from this foreword to a newfound way of thinking and performing. Your work, your life, and your being will never be the same.

When sharing with and advising companies on theatre I often recommend the business film "Fish!" about the wonderful performers at Pike Place Fish Market in Seattle, because each of the four principles it spells out are really acting techniques. From now on I am going to add to that

Steve DRaGroove's (told ya'!) book SING. And what one of the workers says in "Fish!"—"It's not about the fish", it's about your work on your stage—applies here as well. It's not about the karaoke, it's about your work on your stage and in your life. You don't have to like the idea of getting up in front of a roomful of folks and belting out a ballad. (I've never done so myself. When I sing at church people sometimes compliment me, but my wife Julie says it's not because I'm good, it's because I'm loud.) But you can learn from those who do (including the people in the personal stories Steve shares with us), and from the Karaoke Jockey himself who brings out their best.

In keeping with the style of SING, I tried to keep this foreword bite-sized so you can move on with your main task right here, right now—listen to the good Groove Doctor, heed his lessons, and walk away inspired. And, perhaps, humming a tune.

B. Joseph Pine II
Co-Founder, Strategic Horizons LLP, Aurora, Ohio
Co-author, *The Experience Economy*, *Infinite Possibility*, and *Authenticity*

Prologue

 An Unexpected Performance

The crowd shouts out her name. "Karen! Karen! Karen!"

She sits nervously in the booth, shaking her head in protest. It's no wonder the shy brunette wearing glasses and a frozen-food convention laminate feels out of place. She and her work friends definitely stand out dressed in their business attire. Everyone in the dark bar around them is dancing and shouting along to loud music. Finally, after her coworkers repeatedly try to coax her away from the table, Karen takes the stage. As the karaoke track begins to play, she starts to sing Jewel's song, "Who Will Save Your Soul?" and the whole room changes.

"She sounds like Jewel!" a woman says. Others agree— Karen has talent. "I think it's the first time that there's ever been an encore here," one man remarks.

"It was, um, pretty off the charts there," another says afterward, shaking his head in disbelief.

"Every person was like 'Wow, that girl is really good. She shouldn't be here,'" a woman says with a shrug.

"She's got an unbelievable voice," a man says, looking back at the stage. "I'll be honest, I would like to hear her sing again."

"I just thought she had been a professional," a woman says, "but they told me she only sings at Christmas parties."

What the crowd didn't know was that Karen was actually Jewel in disguise. The comedy group Funny or Die[1] had dressed her up in corporate businessperson attire with a prosthetic nose, glasses, and a brunette wig. They challenged her to sing her own songs at The Gas Lite Karaoke Bar in Santa Monica, California to see if the patrons could recognize her underneath her less-than-glamorous persona. They captured it all on camera and posted it on the internet. The result was that Jewel got a whole room of strangers shouting out a name—Karen.

"I don't want to tell Jewel," one man admitted, "but the girl that was singing her song may have actually been slightly better."

Karen the frozen-food rep won over the crowd and made some new fans by giving an extraordinary performance from an unexpected source. This is the power of karaoke—it contains within it an inspiring and unifying force. It brings us together around what we love. For many karaoke singers, it's about the love of music—a love that changes the way you look at the world.

Introduction

 Serious Fun

To the uninitiated, karaoke may seem unappealing. After all, public speaking continually shows up as one of the most common and intense phobias, so singing in front of a crowd may inspire the same stage fright. Yet each of us has a leisure activity or interest that makes us "light up." These are the activities we complain that we don't have enough time for, the hobbies we daydream about during the boring moments at work, the topics we tend to drift toward in our everyday conversation.

The truth is, talent aside, neither Karen, nor Jewel, nor any of us need to be professionals at the things we love in order to get the most out of them. It takes a change in how we think and what we do to break the pattern of dissatisfaction.

Getting No Satisfaction

According to a story published in *Forbes* Magazine, the majority of people are less than satisfied with their jobs. *Forbes* cites a survey by Right Management in 2012 that asked 411 workers in the United States and Canada about their overall job satisfaction. Only a slim 19% of the workers reported that they were satisfied with their jobs, while 16% reported that they were "somewhat satisfied." Even worse, 21% reported that they were "somewhat unsatisfied" and a whopping 44% claimed to be outright "unsatisfied."[2]

This is not good news for the workplace. Jobs are not providing workers with a sense of enjoyment or fulfillment, and the morale of entire companies, families, and communities is at risk.

With the commonplace disconnect between what we do and what we love, something has to change.

Jewel noticed something peculiar about The Gas Lite.

"It was a really unusual place," she said. "They were taking their karaoke very seriously."

Are we ready to take our fun seriously? In this book, I invite you to explore how the concept of loving our play can change our thinking, our doing, our lives—and maybe even the world.

Taking Care of Business

Job dissatisfaction is an epidemic, but it is not without a cure. Finding work that is meaningful requires us to ask below-the-surface questions that lead us toward greater purpose. The process begins with self and moves outward. When we dig deep enough, most of us will find that our sense of purpose is closely tied to what motivates us. If we begin to discover the motivating forces in our lives, we can begin to discover what is truly meaningful to us.

In order to understand what motivates us, we have to ask ourselves, "What purpose do I serve in life—not just for myself, but for others?" It's a community concern. While we strive as individuals to find meaning in work and in life, we find that a vital part of this process is cultivating the desire to share resources, knowledge, time, and wealth with others. If we can gain a deeper understanding of our own motivations and what makes life meaningful for ourselves, we can begin to reach out and share the vision with others. Sharing makes our own dreams bigger in the process.

It can start small with the personal goals that set the stage for our bigger dreams. Many of us want to figure out how to rise above our current station in life. Perhaps we want to provide for our family above all else. Maybe we daydream of taking a vacation or making a major purchase. As we set these kinds of goals, they change the way we move forward. Goals feed our sense of aspiration as we achieve them. In addition to achieving what we set out to gain, these small accomplishments will also help make us more active dreamers.

It's not a hopeless cause. It is possible to find meaning in work, but to paraphrase a quote often attributed to Albert Einstein, the definition of insanity is to do the same thing over and over while expecting different results. To change our level of satisfaction with the workplace, we must first find a way to gain more satisfaction from the rest of life.

Working for the Weekend

Vocation is what we get paid to do. Avocation is what we do that's

worth paying for. Perhaps you live to
play a sport, go to the movies, read a
favorite author, or get outdoors in your
free time. You clock out of the job and
rush to the experiences that make the
rest of the 9-to-5 grind worthwhile.

Avocation can be defined simply as a delight-directed activity we pursue because we want to—not because we have to.

It may seem selfish to you to prioritize
leisure over productivity, but avocation
does not have to be self-serving. Even though our interests start
with ourselves, they can move us outward to enrich the lives of
others around us. Our avocational activities allow us to give of
what we have learned and what we care about to others. They
drive us to spend time with people who are already important to
us and with people we want to get to know better. We can discover
ways to share common interests and passions with others through
pursuing passions and interests of our own.

Avocational activities encourage us to explore things
we might never consider doing for financial reward. We do
them simply because we enjoy them. Baseball enthusiasts
speak about playing "for the love of the game," and outdoor
sportsmen feel the "call of the wild." These non-work pursuits
can teach you to recognize which aspects of work you enjoy.
Once you have identified the enjoyable parts of your vocation
through enjoying your avocation, you can begin to move from
drudgery to meaningful work.

I Can See Clearly Now

Sometimes the process of self-examination will yield
disappointment. Perhaps you had high hopes about your

choice of career, but years later, your responsibilities weigh heavily on you. Maybe the culture of your workplace fails to inspire you, and your day-to-day reality never manages to excite you. It can be painful to take a closer look only to realize the ways your plans and pursuits have let you down. It's easier to turn a blind eye to disappointments and just try to move on with life as it is.

Yet it's valuable to examine the course of our lives and take inventory of what we've accomplished along the way. There are important questions that can help us better understand what's really going on under the surface. How are we doing in the process of reaching our goals? Are we truly prioritizing the things that matter most to us? In what ways (if any) do our interests outside of work influence the choices we make?

Questions like these reveal helpful guides or "signposts" that direct our future actions. When we take the time to uncover these signposts by asking self-examining questions, we reach a fresh perspective and new set of goals. The result is that our sense of vocation—especially regarding work that is disappointing or unsatisfying—will undergo a dramatic shift toward a better future.

A Change Would Do You Good

One of the saddest things to witness is a person despairing because they cannot see the way out of their circumstances. They do not feel hopeful that things can improve into a brighter future. They need

The catalyst for change in our circumstances is dissatisfaction with the status quo. We begin to recognize that there is a better way.

a new perspective that everyday work cannot provide. It is in avocational pursuits that the fresh perspective can begin to develop and flourish, moving each of us—the despairing worker included—outward and away from the same old disappointments and dead ends.

Karaoke is a perfect example of an avocation that can help you identify which "delightful" aspects of work deserve a second look. Singing on the karaoke stage changes your point-of-view by taking you out of your comfort zone, shaking up the ordinary, and breaking you out of complacency with the status quo.

Avocation, like karaoke itself, is not always serious. It can be lighthearted, funny, risky, or even absurd. Avocation is the best avenue for discovering these fun aspects of our goals and aspirations. This aspirational delight can show up as an unexpected feat, like President George H.W. Bush's decision to skydive on his 90th birthday. Avocation allows us to not just think outside the box, but to act outside the box.

Spotlight: My Story

I've shared the stage with some of the biggest names in music—Frank Sinatra, Billy Joel, Elton John, Lynyrd Skynyrd, Ray Charles—stage legends and rock stars alike.

Of course, they were only there in spirit.

In reality, I was alone under the stage lights, belting out their hits with a microphone in hand and the words flashing across the screen on the monitor beside me. Some might call this madness. I call it karaoke night.

Years into my career as a consultant and trainer, I knew I

could speak confidently in front of large, diverse, and even hostile crowds. But singing in front of an audience was an altogether different challenge.

It's not like I'm shy. I was raised the oldest child of two natural-born salespeople, neither of whom had ever met a stranger. I started singing with them in the car on long road trips when I was five years old, harmonizing through the catalogues of Nat King Cole, Perry Como, and the Beatles. They instilled a love of music in me from an early age, but I felt intimidated by the idea of actually performing solo. There's a certain vulnerability about singing in front of people that can be even more nerve-wracking than public speaking. Nobody wants to be the person who comes in at the wrong time or can't hear the cue from the band and gets unceremoniously booed off the stage.

The intensity of that fear kept me in the audience for years.

Yet the inspiration had sparked inside me. I grew up in the 1960s, a period of great turbulence from which some of 20th century America's most inspiring voices emerged. Politicians and world leaders had the dynamism of rock stars, leading the public audience toward a new world of possibilities. I heard the voices of John F. Kennedy, Martin Luther King, Jr., Billy Graham and John Lennon challenging the status quo and reinventing the mindset of a nation. Their voices crying out in a time of turmoil spoke forth a brighter future, breathing life from the podium or stage through the radio and television speakers.

Over time, I became a fan of the great crooners and balladeers who could sing with such ease. Their work transported me to a place where the world seemed at peace and anything seemed possible. My music-loving aunt was a regular concert attender and a big influence on my musical taste. My brother, two sisters and I listened as she would spin singles and LPs in her Indiana living room. We were mesmerized by the rock and roll sounds of The Beach Boys, Elvis Presley, The Beatles, The Birds, and Herman's Hermits, just to name a few of our favorites.

As a high school and college student, I took part in traveling ensembles and competitive choirs. But as much as I enjoyed performing in a group, I could never work up the nerve to confidently sing a solo. These early brushes with musical performance created in me a growing—and sometimes nagging—desire to take the stage on my own. It wasn't until years later, when I first stepped onto the business stage, that I learned how essential the performance mindset is to success in any and every area of life.

More Than a Feeling

Aspiration is the burning desire inside a person that says "I want to be more, know more, give more." It is highly personal. You cannot just place aspiration inside someone else. We all have to go through this process on our own. The first step is self-examination. Are we happy at the moment with who we are and where our life is heading? We may ask "If I could live my life over again, would I make the same choices?"

Likewise, each of us must determine how we measure success. What am I willing to do to achieve my aspirational goals? Am I willing to make the changes required to remove the roadblocks to my dreams? This self-examination may feel awkward, and seem abstract, but it's very practical. Defining and measuring our own concept of success enables us to be more constructive. We can begin to approach goals in a more tangible way. If we have a practical understanding of success, our dreams become attainable. In this way, practicality is not the enemy of dreaming but rather the hands-on strategy that can help us achieve our dreams in real life.

All Fired Up

Where to begin? By thinking differently. The first step in making a change is to overcome the fear of change. This is a challenge that all of us encounter at some point in life. Even for outgoing people, overcoming the fear of change can be daunting. Learning to face this fear in small ways can train our minds to approach other, bigger fears with a greater sense of confidence and purpose.

There's a risk involved with going on stage. You can be rejected, embarrassed, and met with apathy or a lukewarm response. It's much easier to sing in the shower or in the car, safely away from an audience or *Karaoke gives ordinary people an extraordinary opportunity. It allows them to take that first small step toward facing their fears and insecurities.* any objective critique of your abilities. Yet there's a significant change of mindset that comes from taking that risk. You begin to surprise yourself with fearlessness—and not just on karaoke night. The newfound confidence you gain from taking the stage can utterly transform your approach to countless challenges in life. It's an amazing process—both to experience for yourself and to witness in other people's lives—

and it all starts with following your aspiration. Like kindling for a fire or fuel for a vehicle, aspiration is the driving desire that pushes you further than the superficial barrier of your own self- consciousness.

Thus, the purpose of this book. We can all find new aspirations to carry us in the direction of our dreams. We can all explore ways to stretch ourselves to think differently, act confidently, and enjoy life more fully. When we do, our lives will SING.

A Note about the Book's organization

SING! Business and Life Lessons from the Karaoke Stage is organized into 4 Sections, which divide the 100 lessons and motivations. Each section begins with a primary lesson I learned from the karaoke stage, and is followed by 20 to 25 other important lessons (each alliterated with the primary lesson as a means of organization).

S – **S**tep Up is the first lesson for successful performance.

I – **I**nspire and be Inspired. This lesson focuses on finding a source of inspiration and inspiring others.

N – Find your **N**exus—a group of likeminded people to invest in.

G – **G**o for it! Put the lessons to work on your life stage.

Spotlight on Clay: Tech-Guru and Natural-Born Stage Performer

What was perception of karaoke before you tried it?
I knew very little about it, if anything, because I started it right after I turned 21. The first place I ever went to see karaoke, I sang.

Tell us about your first time singing. Who got you into karaoke?
In college, I lived in an apartment complex a good distance from campus, so most of my neighbors were older with kids. My across-the-hall neighbor, a part-time musician, knocked on my door on Sunday evening and asked me if I wanted to go down to the Days Inn to sing. I thought, "Why not? I had never sung solo before—just some musicals in school." It was a rather dingy hotel bar with a Waffle House connected to it. But I remember singing "Raindrops Keep Falling on My Head" and being hooked.

What linkage do you see between doing fun well and doing better work?
I firmly believe that people need to balance. A broad array of interests helps you connect to people, expand your mind, and keep your spirits up. When you are connected and cheerful, you do better work.

What are your "go-to" songs and why?
I have a voice for old country. And while I ran a karaoke show for a year or so in college and learned to expand my range out of necessity, if I only get a few chances to sing I'll usually go to my standards. "You Never Call Me By My Name" by David Alan Coe; "Family Tradition" by Hank Williams Jr; songs by Waylon, Willie, Johnny Cash. Those are the artists I mimic the best.

What, if anything, has karaoke taught you about yourself?
It's taught me that I love the stage. I relish the applause. I don't know if it's that I just love entertaining, or if I love that people enjoy the output of something that I'm passionate about.

What parallels have you observed between karaoke and other areas of your life?

Sometimes it's easier to stick with your comfort zones, but you don't grow and expand if you don't keep adding to your repertoire.

What do people think about karaoke? Do you agree or disagree with their perception?

I think my friends are split pretty evenly between those who love it and those who would rather be hit by a mail truck that go hear amateurs sing.

How do you incorporate fun into your life? What hobbies do you enjoy?

I'm an amateur magician, amateur photographer, and I love stage comedy.

What are the fun aspects of your work life? How do you pursue loving what you do?

I have an opportunity to work with clients in many industries, so I relish being able to learn different businesses. I often have a chance to stand up and speak—another opportunity for the stage.

What do you think the karaoke experience offers people? What do you think it gives to you?

It lets ordinary folks get a little feel of what it's like to be a star. Even in your little bar, even amongst your friends. For those that, well, should probably just sing in the shower, it offers them the opportunity to embrace a little fear, to let yourself be vulnerable, let loose and just have fun no matter what anyone thinks.

Sing!

Part I: Step Up

"Ever since I was an introverted kid, I'd get on stage and be able to break out of my shell."
—Beyonce Knowles[3]

What could you accomplish if you were not afraid? Most people are afraid of trying something new or outside of their comfort zone. Staying in your seat is safe. What would it take for you to make that first step toward the life you desire? The following insights and motivations will encourage you to step up, take calculated risks, and begin to gain confidence in your performance—both onstage at karaoke night and on the stage of life.

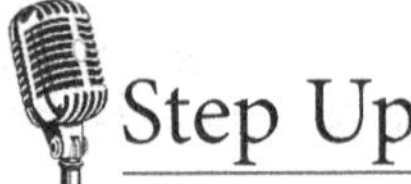# Step Up

When we have a workshop or when we have clients in to work with us side-by- side, eventually we get to the point in the process that's fuzzy or unconventional. And eventually these big-shot executives whip out their Blackberries and they say they have to make really important phone calls, and they head for the exits. And they're just so uncomfortable. When we track them down and ask them what's going on, they say something like, "I'm just not the creative type." But we know that's not true. If they stick with the process, they end up doing amazing things and they surprise themselves with just how innovative they and their teams really are.

—David Kelley, founder of IDEO design firm,
in his March 2012 TedTalk[4]

It's easier to opt out than it is to step up. Opting out because I feel uncomfortable can lead me into a pattern of continually shying away from anything that is uncomfortable. This results in a living a gray existence—one that lacks fun, color, and community—along with all the other things that provide meaning in our life. I see it all the time. People say, "Yeah, that's not for me. You guys can do that—it's fine." It pains me to see when individuals feels like their performance is not worth watching. They figure it's not worthwhile if they're not ready for Carnegie Hall, Madison Square Garden, or a major sporting event's Halftime show.

You know what? That's not what it's about. What it's really about is sharing an enjoyable experience with other people.

Whether you're singing, speaking, or leading a group,

stepping up requires a willingness to share yourself with other people. Nobody can take that risk for you. I'm the only one who can share from my unique set of life experiences. The successes and failures, the celebrations and disappointments, the relationships and acquaintances, the loved ones and strangers I've come into contact with—nobody else can share those but me.

Again, it all starts with changing your thinking. Prominent leadership advisor Mike Myatt recommends putting your life through a "what-if audit"[5] by asking the simple question, "What if…?" When you need motivation to step up to a challenge, start by asking yourself, "What if?" and "What would my life look like if I could?"

The reality is, "can't" never could, and "won't" never will. I attended a church as a teenager where the minister often said, "Too many people in this church suffer from 'can't-sir.'" He went on to say that whenever congregants were asked to volunteer their time to teach or serve in some capacity, they would quickly offer a reason or excuse for saying "no," along with the phrase, "I can't, sir."

A "can't do" attitude often comes from identifying yourself as "just not creative" or "just not good at___________"—you can fill in the blank yourself. You close the book on any possible creative endeavors if you identify yourself as someone who isn't creative. You shut yourself off from excellence if you claim you're fundamentally incapable of excellence.

Stepping up to the microphone is the toughest part. Whether you're talking about literally stepping up to the mike or stepping up to a challenge in any other area of your life, it takes courage. It's moving from knowing in your head that it's the right thing to do to actually putting one foot in front of another until you're at the point of no return. What could you do if you weren't afraid? You've got to step up in order to make it happen. If you keep sitting at the table and daydreaming about how great it's going to be—but you never get up and start to make it happen—guess what? It'll never happen.

 ## Start

I've experienced firsthand how karaoke can build a person's confidence. I've also seen it happen to other people. I've watched dozen of newbies take the stage for the first time. They grip the microphone so tightly that their knuckles go white. They hardly move as the track plays and they can barely eke out a sound. But then over time, something changes. The people who have been so nervous onstage begin to understand how to sync their voice with the lyrics and accompaniment. They become more relaxed and their posture and body language opens up. Over time, they actually began to introduce some principles of showmanship into their performance. And, most importantly, it's obvious that they're having a great time.

It's fascinating to watch because quite often with new karaoke participants, you see a real fear in their eyes. It's much easier to stay seated than to step up and get started. Even confident people are reluctant to get up on stage. Once a person feels comfortable performing in front of a crowd, can read the words in a musical voice *Rather than dreading the moment they're called, the once-reluctant singers look forward to it. Instead of feeling incompetent, they begin to feel confident.*

while they appear on screen, and manages to make it sound like music, their reluctance is replaced by a sense of eager anticipation. You hear people begin to say, "I want my turn to come! I want to get on stage!" There's a huge shift from having to be coerced to actually getting impatient for their chance to sing. Suddenly, they want to hear the KJ (which is short for Karaoke Jockey) call their name.

You're got to stake your claim on the stage. You've got to own your song.

You've got to win over your audience. And those challenges require real confidence and self-encouragement. When you feel you're starting to shrink back, tell yourself: "This is my time. I've stepped up and I'm ready to get started."

 ## Synthesize

Perfect practice leads to perfect performance. One of the most important elements to your preparation is learning to synthesize.

Synthesizing the knowledge and skills you acquire places you on a path to a strong start. In our consulting business, we invest a lot of upfront time in the initial discovery process. We want to be sure we clearly understand our client's needs. The culmination of this discovery process is a recap of our findings—a "rough draft" synthesis. Once we deliver the rough draft, it's reviewed by the client and then returned to us so that we can refine and resubmit it for a second review. The second version—or "revised draft"—that is shaped by the client's feedback is followed by a "final draft"—a presentation and proposal. It's helpful to use a multiple-draft system as often as possible when we're presenting to others. Each round provides a more coherent synthesis than before. We want to make absolutely certain that we present logical, compelling solutions for each client.

Engaging performers on the karaoke or business stage do the same thing.

They create a rough draft—the basic, unpolished idea of what they want to present. Then they refine and revise their performance through strategic practice. Finally, they can deliver a polished version of what they want the audience to hear.

Recently, when I sang karaoke at a local VFW Post, somebody came up to me and said, "You know, you get better at that song every time I hear you sing it." Do I believe that's true? I don't know. But as long as the crowd feels that way— as long as they appreciate it and are energized by it—then I'm on the right track. The audience member's comment was an excellent reminder to me to keep practicing. It's only by continually revising my performance that I can shape it into a spectacular final product.

 # Sprint

Once you step up and get started, you'll be amazed at how quickly you begin to feel confident and inspired. Once your mental barriers are removed, you can begin to sprint ahead at a rapid pace.

For years, athletes generally accepted that running a mile in under four minutes wasn't humanly possible. It all changed when 25-year-old Roger Bannister broke the world record by being the first person to run a mile in 3 minutes, 59.4 seconds on May 6, 1954[6]. there were soon 54 other people who also ran a mile in under four minutes. Once the barrier was broken, the rest of world knew it was possible.

Suddenly, a number of sprinters were able to run the mile faster than four minutes. In fact, within three years of Bannister's achievement, 16 different runners had also clocked sub-4-minute miles. Today, the world record speed is a blistering 3 minutes, 43.13 seconds. This achievement happened because one ambitious individual broke through the barrier. Once he proved it was possible, the rest of the running world knew it, too.

Sprinters often describe their exercise-induced endorphin rush as a "runner's high." When a person gets up on stage and performs well, they experience a similar, almost addictive sensation. Most of us like to be liked, especially when others are watching. Karaoke fuels this sensation. There's the adrenaline, the positivity, the sense of competence, and an overall feeling of accomplishment.

Breaking through your own barrier and achieving a great performance gives you a new positive sense of your own abilities.

 ## Second Impression

Many people make the mistake of thinking that first impressions are everything—both in the business world and the karaoke stage. When you step up and get started, don't forget to think about all the opportunities you'll have to make an impression after the first. Refuse to become satisfied and complacent. Continue to up your game. Sometimes the second impression, final act, or encore can turn out to be the most memorable. As business leader Richard Branson notes: "The first impression is everything. So is the second."[7]

Ask yourself:

- What are some examples of times I didn't make a great first impression, but made a far better second—or third, or fourth—impression?

- How can I learn to make a strong second impression and improve my follow-up with people I meet and performances I give?

- What might people miss in their first impression of me that I should try to convey or communicate in their second impression of me?

 ## Stage Fright

The famous observational stand-up comic Jerry Seinfeld once pointed out that people's number one fear is public speaking. "Death" is number two. Does that sound right? This means to the average person, if you go to a funeral, you're better off in the casket than giving the eulogy."[8] It's another way of saying that that most of us have stage fright. Fortunately, there are ways we can get over this crippling fear of public performance with practice and a little guidance.

Often when I'm at karaoke night, people sit down beside me and ask, "What song should I do?" I may have absolutely no idea what song they would sing well, in which case I'll pick out a song that's relatively simple. I'll usually suggest a selection that they could perform fairly easily based on the songs they like or are comfortable singing. Sometimes I'll ask if they have a favorite song because people will typically sing along to their favorite when they hear it whether they realize it or not. On occasion, I'll even suggest that someone get up on stage with me or to do a group-sing with friends on a crowd favorite like Jimmy Buffett's "Margaritaville" or Aretha Franklin's "Respect."

The key is to avoid suggesting something too difficult, but rather to find something familiar and comfortable. This allows the unsure performer to more comfortably step up onto this strange new performance space: the stage. Once you get someone on stage that first time, it's very easy to get them on stage a second time! The initial goal is to "break the ice" and help them get started on a path to overcome their fear-driven reluctance to perform.

It's a wildly popular fallacy that you can reach a point where you have absolutely zero stage fright. I've talked to a lot of great performers over the years, and whether they're excellent singers, sales presenters, or other types of entertainers, most will admit that there's quite often a small part of them that is still nervous in front of a crowd—even after years of practice.

You may think, "I'll never be scared to speak in front of a group again! I'll always be confident!" But every once in a while, something just creeps in there. Your heart beats a little faster, or you feel a twinge of anxiety or a few butterflies in your stomach. Remember that this can be a healthy thing. We're all human, after all.

We're all vulnerable, and we all have to convince ourselves on occasion that we're capable of excellence and worthy of being onstage.

A little bit of stage fright is a good thing. It gives you that extra adrenaline boost and makes you feel excited. What has to happen to each of us in order to perform well is for us to convert that debilitating stage fright into an artistic edge. You can convert the fear into energy. Seasoned performers make the most of stage fright, transforming the fear from a paralyzing factor into an energizing factor.

Repurpose the emotion.

 ## Self-Editing

We stop ourselves from doing things. We self-edit as we're having ideas. And in some cases, our desire to be original is actually a form of editing.

—Tim Brown, "Tales of Creativity and Play" TedTalk[9]

Sometimes I see people who get upset onstage when they miss a particular note or nuance. Perhaps they failed to slide on a particular note the way the artist did on the original studio recording. Maybe they missed their entrance cue. When this happens, I remind them that 99 times out of 100, the audience does not notice—unless the performer draws an inordinate amount of attention to the mistake. The audience is not that focused. It's a far bigger deal in the mind of the performer than it is in the mind of the audience or client. They'll almost always cut you some slack.

Give yourself the freedom to play, explore, and have fun in the spotlight.

Too much self-editing leads to shutting down your creativity, energy, and optimism.

 # Sizzle

Picture this. You get up on the stage and step up to the mike. You get all the words synched with the background vocals and accompaniment. You give a performance, but you just don't bring your personality. The problem? This is exactly the moment that you've *got* to bring your personality—to bring the sizzle.

Your personality is the only thing you have that you can truly call your own. Everyone has his or her own signature way of presenting. People bring their own unique gestures, vocal style, and distinct persona to the show. That's why you go to see the show in the first place. One Rolling Stone writer described James Taylor's voice as a "clear, vibrato-less instrument as reassuring as a warm fireplace.[10]" Another person who sings with his unusual style would probably not earn 5 Grammy awards, attract millions of fans across the globe, or sell more than 100 million albums[11]. But Taylor has a sizzle all his own. Just like the original "JT," in order to be successful, you must decide to bring your own characteristic sizzle to the stage every time you perform.

 # Spark

Inspiration can come from unusual places. One morning, I had a lightning-bolt moment when I let our dog out of his crate to get his breakfast. I realized as he rushed

Too much self-editing leads to shutting down your creativity, energy, and optimism.

past me that the way he approaches his day is an inspiration to me. Linus, our dog, is an optimist. He is always looking for something to enjoy and always wants his head patted. He often wags his tail. He loves to play with the cat, even though the cat will claw at him and bat him on the nose. He's always upbeat, and he always loves his breakfast of brown crunchy dog food, even though it's the same old brown crunchy breakfast day after day. He thinks it's the best thing ever.

Inspiration often comes from unusual situations. I was inspired by a young man who sings at one of the karaoke venues I frequent. This guy can't carry a tune, but he sells his show so effectively and with such sincerity. He has great stage presence, he plays great air guitar, he knows the words well— unfortunately, he just can't carry a tune. Other than that— arguably crucial—aspect of karaoke, he has the whole thing mastered! And I love to hear him. It's inspiring to me. I think to myself, "I can carry a tune, but what if I got up there with no energy and sucked the life out of the room?" Even without perfect musical ability, that guy's got it going on.

Just as I have, you too can find inspiration in unexpected places. Be on the lookout for the surprising sparks of inspiration all around you.

 ## Stop the Excuses

Okay, so you've stepped up, gotten started—and now it is your time to delight and inspire the audience at home, at work or at karaoke night!

Nobody can make you fail but yourself. I've sung in front of hostile crowds. Believe it or not, some crowds are not very open to the idea of a 50-something-year-old guy with a white goatee and a ball cap getting up and singing in the middle of their hip-hop and rap-dominated evening of karaoke. There's usually some selling and convincing I've got to do. But if I were to let others' opinions keep me off the stage, I would be giving more power to intimidation and excuses than to my desire to step out and have fun.

Stopping the excuses is the start of really enjoying your moment in the spotlight. Don't talk yourself out of an opportunity before you get to really enjoy it. There are times when I have to remind myself that talking about doing something is not the same thing as doing something. Each of us should try to convert the energy we use to make excuses into setting and acting on goals we believe are important to our future.

# Stand Tall

Posture is important. Confidence is important. Your crowd will love you if you love them back. Stand tall in front of them and remember that it's not about you. People want you to be confident, competent, and persuasive when you present.

A successful performance starts with our thinking. If you are willing to break free from fear and get up to perform in front of a group, you have opened up the possibility of dramatically changing your life. You might have lived in fear of standing tall because you are not a highly trained professional performer—you may not even be used to singing around a piano with family or friends. But if you can stand tall and deliver, you're on your way to succeeding as you take on other challenges in life. Things that might have seemed intimidating suddenly seem possible.

You can frame things in a different perspective once you've been able to overcome one challenge in your life—something that was holding you back due to fear. All our challenges in life are connected. I've seen the truth of this in karaoke. People who were afraid to get up in front of a group experience tremendous freedom once they do it. I've heard people tell powerful stories of how this freedom translates into other areas of life such as work, home, and relationships. If you stand tall, people will listen.

 Send a Message

We all have a story to tell and a message we want to communicate. When I hit the karaoke stage, my message is, "This performance is the highlight of the evening. I dare you to top it." I give it everything I've got. Why not? I've got a microphone, after all. When I get in front of a crowd, the one thing I want them to do is to remember that I was there. And the next time I get up, I hope they're going, "All right, that guy's up again! Let's see what he can do."

Quite often, crowds may think you're a one-hit wonder. They think you're a person with one song he can sing or one little shtick he can do. But if you can move from Frank Sinatra to Stevie Wonder to Maroon 5, back over to Ray Charles—and maybe throw some Bonnie Raitt in there to surprise them—you're putting on a show.

People don't know what to expect, but they do know they're going to be entertained. And they know it's going to be worth their time. I think an important message is, "I'm not going to waste your time. You may or may not like my choice of songs. You may or may not like my voice. But I'm going to do everything I can to make sure you're entertained while I'm up here. I'm going to put it all out there." My message is important to me, so I want to send it out with passion and conviction every time I have the chance.

 # Shout

Don't be timid. The world is a very cold and unfriendly place for timid people. Timid people shrink. Timidity can lead to resentment of yourself and others—and ultimately to depression. It's frustrating to feel like no one hears you or that they wouldn't care about what you have to say. Keeping quiet because you're worried about what others think of you is no way to live. Step up and make your voice be heard by those around you. Don't stuff it down. No one else can say what you have to say in the way you say it.

Your voice is unique. Your message is important. Don't let others silence you.

You have a voice—one of the best, simplest and most frequently overlooked tools for sending a message to others. Once you know what you have to say, shout it out! The karaoke stage provides you with a ready venue for sharing your heart and exclaiming your message to the audience. Getting loud is not only tolerated, it's expected and even encouraged. There are times when we all just crave the release of shouting out our feelings, and the karaoke stage is a perfect place to indulge that impulse. Find a great party song or power ballad and allow yourself to let loose!

Share

Seasoned performers often speak of having a vision for how they want to share a particular song, speech or other performance piece. This is how they craft and deliver work in their "signature" style.

As a performer on the stage of life, business, or karaoke, you have to understand the vision for yourself in order to share it with other people. If you know specifically what it is that you're trying to accomplish, the chances are much greater that you'll be able to convince other people to at least consider your point of view. When you are vulnerable enough to share in an authentic way, people will be more willing to hear what it is you feel is important enough to take up their time.

You've got to remember that people are only initially giving you five or ten seconds. They'll either "click off" and go back to their conversations, or they'll lock into what you have to say. The opportunity passes by extremely quickly. If they trust you with their one completely un-renewable, irretrievable, finite resource—which is their time—then you've won them over, and you've really accomplished something remarkable.

Shower Thinking

Admit it—you've probably sung in the shower at some point in your life. Belting out a power ballad while shampooing your hair may annoy your spouse or roommates, but it also may actually serve a useful purpose. Snatching small amounts of time within your routine to sing or just think through things can help you gain confidence for those times when your performance really matters. Often when I take a shower, I may break into song and it seems that along with the flow of water, a flow of ideas begins. Now are all these shower-born ideas or song renditions great? I don't know. I don't write my ideas with soap on the glass, but I try to remember as many of them as I can. While scrubbing your face and washing your hair, you might think of things you normally wouldn't. Movie director, writer and actor Woody Allen claims to have benefitted from shower-thinking as well. He says, "In the shower, with the hot water coming down, you've left the real world behind, and very frequently things open up for you."[12] That brief time of solitude can bring about intriguing ideas.

Don't limit yourself to the shower though! Any moment of alone time throughout your day can be a great opportunity for letting your creativity flow. Engage in "shower thinking" on your morning commute, while you exercise, or on a break from the daily routine.

What times can you harness for some imagination and creativity?

What ideas do you come up with when you let your mind wander freely?

Besides writing with soap on the glass, what ways can you think of to capture these ideas?

 ## Shift

There's something inspiring about breaking routine. It can kick-start creativity in surprising ways. Sameness is the enemy of creative thought. If you never break a routine and always do things exactly the same way, nothing changes for the better. As Albert Einstein famously said, "If you always do what you always did, you will always get what you always got."[13] Your audience gets bored by the same old stuff. We all need to change things up from time to time.

The need for a shift in routine is especially true for those who think they can't do something new or think it feels stupid to be spontaneous. Several years ago, I was leading a sales training in the Chicago area. During these trainings, we always had some type of evening activity to serve as a team-building or bonding time. This particular year, I proposed that we all go bowling. You would have thought I had said we were all going to go have our fingernails pried off. Everybody objected. "Oh, we don't want to bowl! That's stupid! Nobody wants to bowl!" they protested. But you know what? It was absolutely phenomenal. People were so engaged. I really believe it had as much to do simply with the time they spent together and the friendly competition between teams than it did with the pizza and nachos. Another time we took a group from Pittsburgh to New York City, and we rented a room to do karaoke. This is a group that had never done karaoke before and was notorious for wanting to turn in early. Nevertheless, they were out till well after midnight. People who had never sung in front of other people before got involved and sang—and loved it. The person who sponsored the trip came up to me and said, "You know, you were right. I never would have thought that this would have been a team-building and bonding experience for this group." But it really was.

This simple shift in their routine meetings allowed the teams to connect with one another in new and unexpected ways.

 Sensation

Wear the costume, play the role, get up on the stage, bring the power, and you will be a sensation. Giving others a sense of what you want to communicate—whether it's something funny, exciting, angry, romantic, or heartbreaking—is the unique opportunity you have every time you perform. We should never be afraid to be honest and clear with our emotions onstage. The sensation will come across all the more powerfully if we're fully committed to what we're doing, saying, or singing to the audience.

What do you want your audience to feel?

How do you want your audience to respond to your performance? Who do you want to be when you step onstage tonight?

 Silence

Few things in life are more frustrating than being silenced. Yet so many people willingly allow themselves to be locked into silence, hidden behind cubicles, cloistered behind walls, and do not communicate with each other. They don't take advantage of the strength of their colleagues' imagination, ideas, and creativity. This is something that needs to change. Silence should never be more powerful than our dreams.

Having supportive individuals around us can help us break out of silence and break free from something or someone who has held us back. It might be a person in our life or our past with a domineering personality who tried to convince us that we can't do things. It might be a spouse, a parent, a sibling, a teacher or a boss. Not everybody has the strength of personality or the bravery to overcome the past without the support of someone else.

Karaoke and other avocational activities can provide us with a group of friends and a community to lean on that can help us recognize the value of our own voice. As a result, people who have never believed in our own potential begin to develop courage. It can give us that push we need to go, perhaps for the first time. It can challenge that status quo or even change a negative self-image that's been foisted upon us.

 ## Satisfaction

Hanging out with your friends, standing tall, performing to the best of your ability, getting your message out—all of these personally and professionally rewarding goals result in a strong sense of satisfaction. It's because you know you've done your part as a performer, friend, and audience member. You've managed to create a good show and help others have a good time. That's what it's all about.

Once you've done something you once found intimidating, you know for the rest of your life that you can do it. That's a very satisfying realization. The first couple of times I tried singing karaoke, I was scared to get up on stage. After I got confident on stage at one or two locations, I would get scared again trying out a new location. It was a new audience, a new sound system—new everything—and I was afraid to get up and sing. But after several years of successful performance, it became a source of satisfaction. Learning to not take myself too seriously—while still learning to take my craft seriously—taught me that I could sing in just about any situation.

And I have sung in all sorts of unexpected circumstances—when the lyrics went out, when the music didn't work properly—but no matter what, it turned out okay. At the end of the day, it's just karaoke. It's the same way when you get up in front of a group of any kind. If you're there, and you know your material (and they don't), it doesn't have to be perfect. You can have the satisfaction of knowing you gave it your best shot.

Your voice is unique. Your message is important. Don't let others silence you.

Shortcut

While there are no guaranteed shortcuts to success, there is a proven faster way to connect with your audience. Famed storyteller and creator of the story-theatre method, Doug Stevenson, says that "emotion is the fast lane to the brain."[14] If you want to take a short-cut to get inside people's heads and hearts, bring a great show. Be emotional. Don't be afraid to share what's on your heart and what you're feeling. Don't be afraid to share freely from your own life experience and bring out songs that have been particularly meaningful to you. If you do, you'll win over the people who matter most.

Script

Just like an actor in a theatre, I follow a certain script every time I step on the karaoke stage. When I put on the cap and wear the costume and go into the place, I'm not Steve, I'm Doc—otherwise known as the "Groove Doctor." That's who I am. That's my identity. When I'm in the karaoke venue, I think, WWDS—"What Would Doc Sing?" I have to deliberately think, "How would Doc answer that?" I'm not as interested in what Steve would say. Whatever Doc would say or sing is what people expect to hear.

When Doc is on stage—or as they say, "The Doctor is in the house"—I have to put on that persona. I want to make sure I don't violate my Groove Doctor persona because to do so would be inauthentic. If Steve gets up and sings karaoke, it's not the same show. In fact, I've had people say before, "Doc, where's your hat? We've never seen you not wear your hat."

I'm following the script. I play it exactly straight because it is a reality. For my audience, that's what they expect and I don't want them to be disappointed.

 ## Serious Fun

Once you've started, it's time to play. Lego has workshops they call "Serious Play."[15] Some people might consider that an oxymoron. On the one hand, karaoke is a complete farce and total play. On the other hand, it's serious. For one thing, it's cathartic. It's also community-building. It's an opportunity for relieving stress. It's an activity that anyone can do, so it's accessible to a broad range of individuals. It's play but it's serious, too, because there are benefits to participating in it. It helps me tremendously if I've had a tough week just to go sing a few songs, see some familiar faces, and hear them sing. I always feel better at the end of the evening.

Some of the most fun I have at karaoke happens when I'm being playful and singing songs that people wouldn't expect from me. I don't do inappropriate or vulgar songs, just playful ones that make people go, "Oh, I can't believe you did that! That was really funny. What a great song." Sometimes I'll even put on sunglasses if I'm donning a certain persona, or I'll change up my hat to see if people notice. Egging people on, getting up and taking their picture, putting a lighter app on my smart-phone and swinging it back and forth when somebody's singing a particularly meaningful ballad—all these playful actions help create a fun audience experience just for them.

 # Synch

Just as you have to synch your voice with the lyrics on the karaoke screen, it's important to align your goals with the resources you need to succeed.

In my business, I'm always striving to deliver greater value to my customer.

Instead of just trying to get a bigger slice of the pie, I'm interested in creating a bigger pie. In other words, I want to expand opportunity. At some point, I may realize that are some offerings I'm unable to deliver. The best thing I can do if this happens is to align them with someone who can give them what they need, not to do a poor job for them so I can maintain their business. If I disappoint them, I will ultimately lose their business because I've lost their trust. This would be a major error in timing, and it would throw my whole approach out of synch. It's important to develop a trust relationship with my client and an understanding of what I can do and can't do.

At the same time, I need to understand that there are people who have some skills, talents, knowledge and contacts that I don't have. Synching up with them is simply connecting the dots of my bigger picture. It's a way of making sure I'm open to opportunities and gaining a broader perspective. Aligning with others helps me synch up my actions with my goals.

To bring it back to karaoke night, there are certain genres that I don't perform. It's not because I don't like them, but because they don't fit with my life experience or line up with my comfort level. I won't be doing any Mariah Carey or Jay-Z anytime soon. It doesn't mean I can't appreciate the original artists or karaoke singers who perform their songs well. It's exciting to hear others sing selections outside of my personal repertoire. I wouldn't attempt "Rebel Yell" by Billy Idol that my son-in-law sings with great enthusiasm, but I appreciate it when he does it.

The point is to continually synch all elements together into a cohesive and powerful performance. We achieve this when we identify our weakness and begin to align each performance with our strengths.

 ## Stardom

Some people pursue karaoke in hopes that it will somehow lead to them being "discovered" and usher them into a life of fame and fortune. I've got nothing against chasing fame, but it's not for me.

There's a little boy who lives across the street from our home. For his seventh birthday he got a basketball goal. His father and grandfather were soon out there shooting baskets with him. I'm sure this kid has dreams of being Lebron James. Will that level of fame and fortune happen for him? It might sound harsh of me to say it, but the odds are pretty slim. None of us are completely immune from the allure of stardom, and we often feel its pull from an early age.

Occasionally I'll encounter people who are singing karaoke in preparation for the imaginary world tour. It reminds me of a line from the movie "Dumb and Dumber." When the woman Jim Carrey's character loves tells him his chances of getting a date with her are one in a million, he says, "So you're telling me there's a chance."[16] Delusions of grandeur? Check.

Express your passion. Don't attach a financial incentive to everything you do.

Don't spoil something you enjoy by making it into a "fame and fortune" thing. If I were a country singer, I'd write a song called, "I Just Want to Be Rich, I Don't Want to Be Famous." From what I can see from the outside, and based on the few brushes I've had with people who are famous, fame is overrated. You lose your private life, people are always in your face, and you develop this strange expression that says, "Do you recognize me?" Besides, if you're doing something because you love it, the reward is greater than fame and fortune. You can take that to the bank.

 ## Success

You can feel the electricity in the room whenever someone delivers a standout performance. People turn their heads and take notice. Yet standout performances don't just happen.

Success is the culmination of many factors, especially hard work. Stepping up and pursuing success is a risk many people are afraid to take.

Sometimes I wonder—do most people really want to be successful, or do they just want to talk about what it might be like? There's not just a fear of failure, there's a fear of success. Many seem to ask themselves, "What if I become successful? Will I be able to handle wealth and fame?" Then, after some thought, their answer comes to them, "I don't know! As long as I don't try, I won't have to worry about that!"

Success is a journey, not a destination. Once you've encountered success, you'll want to taste its sweet fruits again and again. The desire for success is what gets people up in the morning—and it really has little to do with financial remuneration. The desire for success is tied to a sense of wellbeing and the confidence that you've done your best. Give freely of yourself, sincerely and openly, and that's all you can do. To me, that is success. If I've been true to myself and authentic in my dealings with others, that is success.

Helping other people gain confidence about what they have to offer others is success. I don't mean throwing out empty praise to make them feel good about themselves. The goal is to actually help them to the point that I begin to see progress in their lives toward becoming a more fully functioning member of their community. Once I reached a certain age and season of life, I began to consider and talk about my legacy—what I'm going to leave behind. A positive legacy is a sign of success. All these things can sound very profound, but in reality, when you look at your life and start doing the math, you begin to say simply, "If others want to benefit from what I've learned and lived through, what can I say to help them?"

True success does not come as a result of being aggressively competitive, but rather attuned to what's happening around us. I don't view other companies in my field as my enemy—as if I'm competing against them and I want to win at their expense. I look at it as if we're all competing on parallel tracks for the same prize. We're all looking forward and investing ourselves in what we do well. We may have similar goals of gaining a new client, a higher level of fulfillment, or a greater level of professional recognition. If they're really good at what they do, there may be an opportunity to form an alliance with them. We may be able to hire them or be hired by them. There may be an opportunity to provide them with a reference to a client who needs something we're not prepared to deliver. They may be willing and able to do the same for us.

Success is not a zero-sum game. It's not, "I win, you lose." Success is, "I know what I hope to accomplish, and I'm going to go after that." It's stepping up to the challenge and availing myself of every resource, every bit of business wisdom, every experience, and every talented or smart person I can find to help me be successful.

 # Song in Your Heart

Delight in the discordant sound of a wrong note—it's leading you to a new song.

—Susan Ann Darley[17]

I love to listen to little children singing. On my most recent birthday, my grandchildren called with their parents from Disney World to sing me "Happy Birthday." My granddaughter's sweet, clear, soprano voice was just so beautiful— and she hit virtually every note, which I found pretty impressive for her to do without accompaniment!

Sometimes I even enjoy hearing people who feel safe and feel confident enough to get up and sing despite the fact that they don't have tremendous skill when it comes to hearing or hitting the right notes. If they have great stage presence, a high level of confidence, and a loud, clear voice (even if it may not be perfectly on pitch), I love to hear them. As long as they're not obnoxious or intentionally sounding bad, there's a certain beauty to it.

I remember attending church as a child with my grandmother. Someone in a nearby pew was singing off-key on a familiar song. I started to snicker, and my grandmother looked sternly at me at me and said, "Singing is not just for those with a great voice. Singing is for those with a song in their heart." What a beautiful statement. If we have a song in our heart, it lifts our spirit. Not just in church, but anywhere— walking down the sidewalk, or even while we're working. Even Disney's Seven Dwarves recognized the value of whistling while they worked.[18] It makes your work lighter. Having that song in your heart is a wonderful way to live.

 # Your Step Up Track List:

1. Shout—The Isley Brothers
2. Say What You Mean to Say—John Mayer
3. I Want You to Want Me—Cheap Trick
4. Stand By Me—Ben. E. King
5. Something to Talk About—Bonnie Raitt
6. New Sensation—INXS
7. Changes—David Bowie
8. Kelly Clarkson—Breakaway
9. Roar—Katy Perry
10. Shine Bright Like a Diamond—Rihanna

What other Step Up tracks are on your list?

____

____

____

____

Rehearsal Notes

1. Are there some areas of your life where you feel that you've been "opting out" rather than "Stepping Up"? List these below.

____

____

____

____

2. What are some of the excuses that have kept you from "Stepping Up" in those areas?

____

____

____

____

3. Identify one of these areas to work on today. Get started. What will be your first step?

____

____

____

____

Spotlight on Dave: Naturally Introverted Market Data Expert Turned Confident Karaoke Frontman

What was perception of karaoke before you tried it?
Karaoke always looked like something that would be fun for other people, but not something I would try. By nature I am an introvert, and the thought of getting up on stage in front of a lot of people I didn't know was terrifying.

Tell us about your first time singing. Who got you into karaoke?
I was introduced to karaoke by a close friend who had been doing it for years—and was so into it that he even had a stage name!

What linkage do you see between doing fun well and doing better work?
I feel that it is possible to do good work without having fun for relatively short periods of time. However, building a career and doing work that one can feel passionate about over the long run is not possible when one doesn't experience joy in what they do. Without having fun, burnout is inevitable—no matter how far one rises in an organization or how much money they make.

What are your "go-to" songs and why?
"Brown-eyed Girl" by Van Morrison is my 'go-to' song. It is in a range that my voice can handle comfortably, it has a great 'feel' that people respond to immediately, and the words paint a vivid picture of a simpler time in our lives.

What, if anything, has karaoke taught you about yourself?
While I am by nature an introvert, there is an extroverted personality within me that wants to break away and be the life of the party and experience the joy of connecting, having fun, and building great memories with people around me.

What parallels have you observed between karaoke and other areas of your life?
In order to grow, it is critical that we step out of our comfort zone. This doesn't mean we need to make radical changes - but always need to be looking for ways to grow and expand our skill set.

I've also seen that everyone has their own unique personality, and that I shouldn't immediately take a disliking to people who are different than me. Everyone has unique skills and personality traits—and while they may be different from mine, I can appreciate and respect them.

What do people think about karaoke? Do you agree or disagree with their perception?
It may be cliché, but I think that many see karaoke as something that exists for Japanese tourists or frustrated "American Idol" dropouts. Before trying it myself, I agreed with this perception, but now I see it much differently. It is a way of expressing oneself and sharing fun with others.
I have always enjoyed listening to music, and spend a great deal of time listening to various styles and artists— everything from Baroque Brass to today's Indie Rock (well, not so much of the Indie Rock, but you get the idea.) I also enjoy learning and read voraciously. And I enjoy sports— both watching and attending, and participating through working out at the gym, hiking, and bike-riding.

What are the fun aspects of your work life? How do you pursue loving what you do?
I am a 'data-geek' by nature, and enjoy any opportunity to use information to help in better running a business, whether

one I am directly involved in, or helping others learn new ways to better run theirs. I pursue this by continually updating my skills and searching for new ways of doing things and proactively sharing those with others.

What do you think the karaoke experience offers people? What do you think it gives to you?
Karaoke offers people the opportunity to search inside of themselves to become more self-aware. Whether learning from the music itself, the reaction of others to their singing, or simply being in a crowd of fun people, it is possible to grow as an individual and help others do the same.

It has given me a higher level of self-confidence, as well as made me more open-minded about others with whom I interact. It has simply made me more willing to see the good in others by helping me see the good in myself.

Spotlight on Linda: A Fun-Loving Middle School Teacher Who Becomes a Kid Again Onstage

What was perception of karaoke before you tried it?
At some point I thought that karaoke was some sort of seedy.

Tell us about your first time singing. Who got you into karaoke?
My friend Tracie convinced me to go out one night in the year after college. We were in Fayetteville, Arkansas and we were on an outdoor patio drinking pomegranate margaritas. I did back-up vocals for "Gangsta's Paradise" and then went on to solo a song by Meredith Brooks.

What linkage do you see between doing fun well and doing better work?
I produce good work when my anxiety is low, and my anxiety is lowered when I laugh, remember that life is short, and remember that I can mess up and still be OK. Being intentional about "fun" is a powerful way to encourage excellence in the professional life.

What is your "go-to" song and why?
"Strawberry Wine" by Deena Carter because I love it so very much.

What, if anything, has karaoke taught you about yourself?
It's taught me to not take myself too seriously. It's helped ease the nausea of public speaking. It's taught me that if I try really, really hard, I can remember the lyrics to a song.

What parallels have you observed between karaoke and other areas of your life?
Karaoke is a chance to see some of the best aspects of humanity. I've been to a lot of karaoke bars over the past

5 years, and I really can't ever recall seeing someone in the audience maliciously making fun of a performer. And some of these performers are terrible! I tend to see friends encouraging one another, and dutifully singing along by the stage while their timid friend performs her first solo. Karaoke offers the chance to see people step out of comfort zones.

What do you think the karaoke experience offers people? What do you think it gives to you?

Karaoke gives adults a chance to look like idiots – the great misconception is that an adult knows what it means to be an adult. The truth is, they don't, and karaoke is one of those things that allows an adult to truly embrace the opportunity to not have it all together.

S**I**NG!

Part II: **I**nspire and be **I**nspired

"What lies behind us and what lies before us are tiny matters compared to what lies within us."
—Ralph Waldo Emerson[19]

Each of us need sources of inspiration, and each of us can become a source of inspiration for others.

The word inspire is a verb that, according to Webster's means "to make (someone) want to do something : to give (someone) an idea about what to do or create." Inspiration leads to motivation. "Wow!" I think this is something I can do for myself—and for those around me.

Do you enjoy learning? I do. For me, learning has become one of life's great pleasures. I find that learning, whether from my own experiences, or from the experiences of others, becomes fuel that energizes me to try new things. Learning leads to inspiration, and inspiration leads to action.

One important life lesson I've learned is that when I continually fill my inspirational tank, I am motivated to pass along inspiration to others. As their "tanks" are filled, they can do the same for others around them, and so on.

Noted motivational speaker, Zig Ziglar reached and influenced an estimated 250 million people with his 33 books, numerous videos and recordings, and many live presentations during his 35 year career. He was once challenged by someone who questioned the value of his message and his methods in seeking to inspire audiences with motivational messages. His response is worth reading and remembering: "People often say motivation doesn't last. Neither does bathing—that's why we recommend it daily." Go forth and inspire yourself and those around you.

 Improvise

I'm still waiting for that moment in life when everything goes exactly like I think it will. But until then, I think it's a good policy to be willing to improvise. People don't know whether you're following the exact script or not unless they wrote it or are reading along with you. Get the gist. Understand the spirit of what it is you're singing, saying, or doing.

Improvisation is a wonderful gift to offer people. It's where some of the world's most memorable performances come from. A lot of people don't know that although the inspirational "I Have a Dream" speech by Dr. Martin Luther King, Jr. was written out, the most famous part of the address, when he talks about "the dream" for his children and the future was not in the original written text.[20] It was an improvisational moment when MLK launched into this beautiful, highly memorable oration. The result was a soaring oratory that people have remarked about with awe for the last 50 years.

Improvisation is essential. Each of us brings a unique set of talent, experience, energy, and personality to any piece of music, speech, or writing. We shouldn't sit on that opportunity. We should allow it to unfold and open up. The whole nature of improvisation is additive. It's "yes, and."

Comedic writer and actress Tina Fey, best known for her work on the TV shows *Saturday Night Live* and *30 Rock* as well as starring roles in movies, started her career as a member of a touring improvisational theatre group. In her memoir *Bossypants*, Fey outlines her "rules of improv" that give a helpful look at what makes improvisation successful. The second "rule" in particular applies to performing, presenting, and practically any area of life in which you must respond to an unexpected moment:

Rule #2 — Not Only Say Yes… Say Yes And

> The second rule of improvisation is not only to say yes, but YES, AND. You are supposed to agree and then add something of your own.
>
> If I start a scene with "I can't believe it's so hot in here," and you just say, "Yeah…" we're kind of at a standstill.
>
> But if I say, "I can't believe it's so hot in here," and you say, "What did you expect? We're in hell." Or if I say, "I can't believe it's so hot in here," and you say, "Yes, this can't be good for the wax figures." Or if I say, "I can't believe it's so hot in here," and you say, "I told you we shouldn't have crawled into this dog's mouth," now we're getting somewhere.[21]

Do you see the additive element at work in these examples? By adopting the "yes and" mindset, you can contribute more to a conversation, presentation, or performance by seizing the opportunity to expand and enhance whatever is happening on its own in the moment. Also, it allows you to connect with other people and their ideas rather than letting the exchange of thoughts and words fall unceremoniously into awkward silence.

Aretha Franklin is a great example of an artist who uses improvisation to inspire her audiences. The song "Respect" didn't include the spelling out of the word. She sang that as a kind of experiment. It was a total improv her sister thought up and that they incorporated on the fly[22].

Many scat improvisations in jazz are totally experimental

as well. Sometimes I'll try things when I'm up on stage. I'll sing during the middle of a musical break, and it really adds to the show and makes it fun. It's fun to try to hit a high note when nobody expects you to. Sometimes it doesn't work out, but you know what? It's okay. We don't allow people to throw rotten tomatoes in any of the karaoke venues, so I'm safe.

It's fun to improvise and experiment. Life is gray if you don't ever try something you're not comfortable doing at first. I actually found out rather late that I love guacamole, as silly as that sounds. For years, I didn't try it because I'd only had bad guacamole that's more like baby-food peas. It was thin and runny and dark green and smelly. Until one day I actually had some fresh guacamole made from ripe avocadoes, and when I tasted it, it was oily and good and flavorful and wonderful. I wondered how I had gone fifty years without knowing that I enjoyed this stuff!

If you want to inspire those around you on an ongoing basis, you've got to be willing to improvise and experiment. We're not pressing a million copies of this karaoke song. It's an ephemeral performance. Somebody might record it and put it on YouTube, but if they do, who am I to stop them, right?

 # Immerse

Creativity and Business coach Susan Ann Darley explained the importance of conquering our fear of failure. In a Huffington Post article titled, "Creativity: Moving Beyond Your Doubts and Fears," Darley says:

> The fear of failure, making mistakes, hitting the wrong notes, can keep us in chains and stifle our

creative exploration. Creative genius emerges from experimenting, trial and error and the willingness to risk.

Like a child, joyously immerse yourself in the moment. Drop the rules and allow your sensibilities to guide you.

Delight in the discordant sound of a wrong note—it's leading you to a new song.

And the next time your fears and doubts begin to cast a shadow on your talents and rob you of your joy, look within. Tap into your intrinsic worth as a human being. Recognize the gift of the life force within you that flows and creates through you.[23]

For years, I've had a recurring dream that puts me back in college on the way to class and, all of a sudden, people tell me it's the final exam and wonder where I've been all semester. In real life, I've experienced similar panic by going into meetings ill-prepared and then suffered the consequences. It's interesting to me that almost always, the fear of what might happen—or what I imagine in the very worst of cases could happen—seldom actually does happen. It's usually not as bad as I think it's going to be.

Sometimes immersing yourself is scary or messy, but that's okay. There's a strange buoyancy that you experience when you throw yourself into whatever your art or work happens to be, wherever it leads you. If you throw yourself into it and totally immerse yourself in it rather than standing back along the edges, you find the buoyancy you never would have experienced otherwise.

I remember jumping 30 feet off a cliff into the murky water at Rock Island State Park and thinking, "Gee, will I die? Will I hit a tree? Will an eagle swoop down and carry me off to its nest on the way down? What will happen?" But I realized that once I jumped in, the buoyancy of the water carried me and I was so inspired, I swam across to go do it again, which was awesome! After jumping in the first time, the second time was easy. Before the first time, I looked over the edge and thought, "Holy cow, I can't step up to this challenge!" All the things that could go wrong or reasons I shouldn't have been there went through my mind. But then once I got started, there was this sense of release and freedom that comes with throwing yourself out there and saying, "I can do this."

It's the same way with perfectionism. We have to immerse ourselves, trust the process, and rely on the people around us. We have to let ourselves believe that if we've prepared, and if it's something we really believe is important, we're going to be okay.

 # Insecurity

Little kids want so badly to grow up. When I was five, I remember asking my grandmother if, when I was ten, I could call her by her first name. I thought when I was ten I would be big. I thought that suddenly, when I was finally ten years old, I would possess this knowledge and worldly wisdom that I didn't have when I was a five year old. Then when you turn ten, you want to be 16, because when you're 16, you can drive a car. Then when you're 16, you want to be 18, or 21, or whatever the next rite of passage is, so you can be considered a legal adult, or join the military, or go to certain shows, and then you want to be 25 so you can rent a car.

And on and on it goes. You imagine that all these magical

things will open up to you in life that you never knew before, and you will miraculously have this insider knowledge that you never had before. More often than not, it doesn't happen. You might be 40 years old and still feel like you did when you were five asking your grandmother if you can call her by her first name. We retain a certain remnant or core to our identity that harbors the insecurity we felt as children. Even if you're insecure when you start to attain the success you seek, you can know that it's a journey—and it's not over. You can keep building your confidence and breaking away from your insecurity with every step forward to who you want to become on the stage and in life.

 # Impostor

I've noticed a common life experience continue to surface in conversations with others. It seems that many of us feel ill-prepared to do our work, to perform a musical number, to speak in front of a group, be a parent, or a spouse, or whatever it happens to be. As we move forward, we may feel that we're a fake or phony. Someone will find us out.

It's okay. We're all human and we're all undertaking the same journey, the same walk. Many of us have the same goal of wanting to create a better world for others. And yet, sometimes we feel like phonies.

Every person, even the ones who have accomplished great things and received tremendous recognition, feels this way from time to time. There are several examples of world-renowned performers and leaders in their field who felt at times like they were a phony. Such notables as actress Meryl Streep, musician

Chris Martin, and Rugby legend Darren Lockyer have all shared that they struggle with a form of profound self-doubt known as "impostor syndrome" at times.[ii] There have been times when I've stumbled and haven't done my best, but is that a reason to give up? No. Giving up is worse than simply not doing your best. Learn from the failures, move forward, gain the skills and knowledge you need, and try again.

I haven't met many people who, when I have an honest conversation with them that reveals a little under-the-surface truth about them, don't also admit that they lack confidence in some area. You know, for someone to say, "I never lack confidence! I always know what I'm doing!" probably means they're a liar, a megalomaniac, or a narcissist. All of us know we're just people. We have successes and failures. We all have to prepare properly, or we all fall on our faces. Bestselling authors know that even though they had a New York Times bestselling book, their next book could be a flop. Great filmmakers make blockbuster movies followed by commercial and critical flops. It's all a process of growth, and the important thing is to keep creating and working through the insecurity. This way, we can move beyond the feeling of being an impostor without letting it hold us back.

 Imperfection

Perfectionism can be paralyzing. It can keep you from leaving the house. It is personality agoraphobia. Just like agoraphobic people are afraid of getting outside or being in crowds and want instead to cower inside their houses with the blinds closed, perfectionists want to hide out in their familiar surroundings where they believe it's safe. When I'm focused on being perfect and acting perfectly, I cannot focus on inspiring others.

Be open and aware. When we keep our eyes open, we observe how life gives us repeated opportunities to try again. You're not going to bat 1,000 every time. Consider the Hall of Fame baseball player. What do you have to do to be in the baseball hall of fame? You have to get a hit about 3 out of 10 times. You have to catch the ball and field the ball properly about 97% of the time. If you do this consistently over a career, you may become a Hall of Fame baseball player. You can at least be an all-star. So flip that around. You improperly field three out of 100 balls that are thrown to you. You strike out or ground out seven out of 10 times. That percentage of imperfection will land you a spot in the hall of fame and immortalize you in sports history.

The truth is, the only person who never makes a mistake is the person who never does anything new, but that's the greatest mistake of all. A missed cue or an incorrect note is not the end of the world. You still have the chance to make an impact. If you're someone who seeks to be inspiring and to be inspired, you have to embrace imperfection.

 Iconic

Icons model what inspiration looks like when it's put into action. Consider some of popular music's most iconic performers. What made them extraordinary? One of the 20th century's greatest stars was Frank Sinatra. What a brilliant example from the musical world of someone who, by Classical standards, didn't have an extraordinary voice. He had a good control of pitch and tone, but not an exceptionally beautiful voice. Yet he made every song his own. He sold over 250 million albums, won 11 Grammy awards,[24] and was a great teacher to others. He didn't mentor others by teaching vocal style, but by finding ways to inspire their artistic creativity and teaching people to have a magnetic stage presence. Sinatra inspired confidence in other performers to believe in themselves and be the very best that they could be. He showed others the vitality of having their own unique sense of style. It's no stretch to believe he was telling the truth when he sang, "I did it my way."[25]

There is much we can learn from icons like Frank Sinatra. Going to karaoke night this week? What can you add to your performance to make it uniquely yours? Presenting in meeting this week? How can you make it memorable?

 # Imagine

Every great achievement began in someone's imagination. Albert Einstein once said, "I am enough of the artist to draw freely upon my imagination. Imagination is more important than knowledge. Knowledge is limited. Imagination encircles the world."[26]

Imagination is an important tool in developing your confidence onstage. One example of harnessing your imagination to reduce your performance anxiety is a set of techniques called NLP, or Neuro-Linguistic Programming. NLP techniques are rooted in theories of communication, psychotherapy, and self-improvement, and demonstrate the power of our minds to affect both our mental and emotional states as well as our actions. The practice of imagining your successful performance in rich, vivid detail will actually—and amazingly—lessen your fears about stepping up to the challenge.[iii]

Imagination is limitless. If you can think it, you can do it. If you can come up with an idea that is original—something that no one has thought of and operationalized before—it can literally change people's way of living. Each of us has an inner child who is ready to imagine. Nurture the little kid inside of you—he can teach you a lot.

How can your inner child help you deliver a better performance?

What ways can you further develop your imagination—and use it to make you a more inspired and inspiring performer?

# Invent

There are new opportunities that have never yet seen the light of day. In order to understand that more fully, look back to recent history. Let's pretend this is 1975. DVRs don't exist and VCRs are $1500. Where are the MP3 players? They don't exist. Where are the DVD players? Where are cell phones? Where's the Internet? That was nearly 40 years ago.

Let's fast-forward 40 years from today. We can be certain that there will be ideas that literally change the way we live, our quality of life, the way we communicate, and potentially everything else. Who knows what stage of development they are in right now, but these exciting thoughts illustrate for us why inventing is so important. People like Nicola Tesla and Thomas Edison made amazing and wonderful contributions, but the inventors of today can, too. I'm sure that at some point I've talked to someone who will be a ground-breaking inventor.

Harness your creativity in a way that will serve your audience at a higher level. If you continue to think about your audience and what they need, you will in turn feed your creativity. That's why I love the name of our company—Solutions. I think about the meaning of that name often. We're not in the problem business. We're in the solutions business.

We're focused on solving. How do you solve things? You get a group of smart, motivated people together. You bring together people who are talented, insightful, and committed to finding answers and meeting needs.

Instead of thinking, "How can I be more creative?" start to think about the people and the needs around you. Invent solutions for them.

Illuminate

The stage lights at a karaoke venue are an interesting phenomenon. They can illuminate the performer, but they can also blind the performer. Your focus should always be on the crowd—not on the lights. The lights are there to create a better show for the audience, not to make you feel attractive and important.

Never get blinded by the spotlight being on you. If I look at it and say, "Wow, I'm up here in the lights," I could easily become less focused on what matters. I could perform a poorer show, and I could get distracted from my real purpose in being there—to put on a great show and inspire the audience. Instead, I look at the lights and other staging elements and think, "This is all part of the show." Likewise, we want to illuminate opportunities for the customer. The key thing is knowing where to shine the light. We're all a part of something bigger that we can illuminate for others.

Instigate

I love to be first in the lineup at karaoke. It inspires others to step up and start. When they see me, they will often say to themselves, "Hey, if that guy can do it, I can do it."

I'm also an instigator at times. I think about the difference between instigating versus initiating. Sometimes you provoke a little teasing and response from people. I like to kind of stir things up. Don't settle for the same old stuff. Upset the apple cart. It helps you break free from the mental bondage and slavery of sameness we can experience if we don't ever try something new.

Instigation can change your whole outlook. It was tough for me to move out of the 70s and 80s and into the more recent 2000s with some of the songs I was doing—or even to attempt country since I didn't grow up being a fan of country music. Over the past few decades of living in Nashville, the capital city of country music, I've grown to appreciate it and even perform it from time to time! I owe some of my karaoke repertoire to the instigators in my own group who continually inspire me to try out new material. Changing things up moves you forward in ways you may never have anticipated.

 Inquire

Ask plenty of questions. How else do you expect to get to know those around you at home, work, or karaoke night? A desire to know more fuels our dreams and ambitions. Curiosity and the ability to ask questions is fundamental to the health of all relationships in life. It's important to learn how to ask questions without having the answer you want to hear tucked away in your mind (while you are seemingly quiet and respectful while the other person answers). Honest listening is vitally beneficial and sadly rare. There's a difference between really having a genuine desire to know and just asking a question to confirm what you already believe. Many people nod along, as if they're just waiting to say, "Now let me tell you what the real smart person has to say!" You'll never know if you never inquire.

Asking others what their favorite song choices are and what inspires them can ignite your own inspiration. Inquiring minds are rarely bored. People who make a habit of continually inquiring are also always finding new questions to ask and gaining fresh perspectives on their own performance.

 # Inoculate

If enthusiasm is contagious, I want to inoculate you with enthusiasm so you can't be brought down. I am the Groove Doctor, and I'm here to make house calls and inoculate people with the love of life and karaoke.

Our emotions are contagious, whether we're enthusiastic or dour, negative or positive in our approach to a situation. It helps to remember that people are watching. We are always on stage, whether it's the personal relationship stage or the business stage or the performance stage, there is an audience of people watching us. Our attitudes are influential. People take note of what we do and say, "Let's participate," or not. "Let's be part of the fun," or not.

There have been many situations that I've walked into where people were very down or negative. By making a conscious effort to generate a positive emotion, I've been able to inspire others and raise the atmosphere in the room up to one of enthusiasm, enjoyment and lighthearted fun. Sometimes it takes deliberately acting in a way that will engage others in positivity and encourage them to look on to the happy side of every circumstance. As the comedians of Monty Python would say, "Always look on the bright side of life."[27]

 # Intimate

Many of us like to keep a "healthy distance" from others, but this can be a major obstacle to making authentic connections. To be intimate is to be vulnerable.

Whenever you get up and perform something only you can do, you are at the same time exposing yourself to ridicule or praise. Whatever the outcome happens to be, there it is. You are inviting either encouragement and praise or ridicule and criticism—you don't really know which will emerge until you do it. We who take the risk of getting up on the stage are opening ourselves up to the comments of others—whether positive, negative, or neutral—so when your turn comes around, give it your best shot. By doing so, you may inspire those around you to do the same.

 # Ideation

Ideation begins with the expression of an individual thought, idea, or perspective. When we share our inspiration, the ideation process begins. Ideation works best when another person is open and willing to listen and share in return. It's a two-way street. I share my idea, you share yours.

A helpful practice of ideation is to set aside an idea time. We have what we call "white board time" in our office. White board time is awesome. We will sketch out whatever we have going on with our current project list. It's both a current project management and future opportunity discussion time.

White board time usually happens on Saturday mornings. We'll take at least an hour or two and white-board and talk about what's currently going on, coming down the road, or what we anticipate. We discuss what clients have brought to our attention, and what we're seeing in the news and around our industry. It's a productive time of synthesizing the news feeds, the projects on our plate, and information I've learned through my contact with people as I'm traveling around the country. We're able to create and think through the process of ideation.

Entrepreneurs understand that when they watch a successful person, whether in the media or out in public, they won't sit back and think, "That's interesting," or "That's entertaining." Instead, they'll think, "How can I create a business opportunity out of that idea?"

That's what ideation is, and that's what we do. We think it out. Another version of this entrepreneurial question is, "How can we serve our client better through what we learned today?" We can only arrive at this question by intentionally setting aside time to develop our ideation. Otherwise, literally dozens or hundreds of great ideas evaporate one after the other and may never see the light of day. It takes that specific span of time. Capture a couple of hours and white-board your best ideas.

 # Intentional

Our actions are guided by our intentions. I always want to adopt a mindset that is purposeful and intentional about respecting others. I want to stay focused on the goal of delivering value for my customer, client, spouse, and everybody involved. I want to remain very intentional about how I say things, what I say, and the type of body language I use. These are all controllable factors. If I go up in front of a group and I'm lazy or ill-prepared and I don't really focus on these priorities, I either put on a bad show or I create a wrong impression. I may convey something other than what I hope to, or just have very little impact on my audience. Intentionality matters.

 # Imitation

If imitation is the sincerest form of flattery, I think building upon that imitation is even better. We all have our personal heroes or people whose style we seek to emulate—people we respect and want to be like. An uninspired karaoke performance can come across as nothing more than a cheap imitation of the "real" version. When we aspire to a higher level of performance, we don't want to just become an imitation of the artist, but to create something new and meaningful from the spring-board of their inspiration to us.

I remember when I was in college, the chancellor of the school dressed in a particular way with a certain color of suit and tie. There were those in the freshman and sophomore class who wanted to be like him, so they began to dress the same way. It was a bizarre phenomenon to see. These folks were walking around with a navy blue suit and a red tie, all dressed like this man who was in a position of leadership. But of course, dressing up in similar clothes didn't really make them like him. They had the imitation down but failed to grow authentically beyond it.

In the same way, when we come into contact with a personal hero or observe a respected person on stage or on screen, we ought to be reminded that we each have our own unique set of giftings and abilities. We bring those qualities to the table as well as whatever we respect or admire about that particular role model or inspiring person. These people can be mentors to us, calling us to be more than mere cardboard caricatures of the real thing.

 Intimidation

It occupies so much of our conscious thought at times that we can fall victim to the intimidation tactics that other people or even our own brains will use against us. Giving in to intimidation is self-sabotage. It will quickly snuff out our creativity and desire to achieve.

Fear is a crippler of creativity and inhibitor of high performance. It keeps us from doing our best.

Whenever I begin to feel intimidated—whether it's when I'm singing, speaking, or presenting in front of a group—I take a few deep breaths and think, "Everyone here deserves the very best I can offer, so I refuse to be intimidated." I'm here for a purpose, and that purpose is to serve others at the highest level possible. I may not have all the answers, but I know that I have a message worth hearing. I need to be honest enough to ask questions when I do not understand and to seek to learn when there's something beneficial I can receive from someone else.

When intimidation creeps in, one of our best resources is other people. I will bring others into the process so I can say, "This is how we—together—can provide the best solution for you."

 Incubation

Good ideas take time to form. Even when I generate a new idea, it may just be one small piece of the idea at a time. For example, I'm really good at thinking of titles of talks or books or movie scripts that I would like to write, but then comes the heavy lifting of fleshing the thing out from start to finish. Obviously, this part of the process takes a great deal more time. In the case of singing a new song, I may hear it on the radio and think, "That's in my range, and I know the song somewhat." But I need to think about it for a while longer than that initial impulse. I need to hear it in the original key and consider the venue I'll be performing it in before my most promising rendition is fully formed.

I perform sometimes at The Mint in San Francisco, which is a karaoke bar open 365 days a year, 3 pm to 2 am. They have hundreds of performers come through to sing every night. There are songs that I might sing at The Mint that might not be well received if I'm singing here in the Nashville area—and vice-versa—or if I happen to be in the Midwest somewhere. It's the same way with presentation audiences. I will present differently to an audience of executives than I will to a group made up primarily of front-line employees. I would need to have some time to allow my ideas to incubate during the planning process and become fully formed before I put my presentation together.

Sometimes I get impatient with the slow-cooker of my mind. I want it to be a high-heat grill. But most of the time, the idea needs time to cook. It's got to simmer. It needs to cure like a great cheese or salami. If you eat an aged food right away while it's fresh, it's a totally different experience than allowing it the time it needs to cure and ripen and become absolutely beautiful and delicious in its character and quality.

I encourage you to look at this developmental time as valuable incubation, not wasteful procrastination. Often there's a fine line between the two. It's easy to say, "Well, I just need to give that more thought," and it never happens. It's like writing a book. "I'm going to get to that next week!" we say, but then where are the pages? Eventually, you have to draw a line in the sand and say, "I'm at least going to start moving forward and putting some action behind my good intentions."

Often the best ideas take time, so trust the incubation process. Just don't let your ideas overcook!

 # Influence

Some of the really rewarding aspects about teaching and mentoring others are those unexpected moments when people approach you and say, "You really made a big difference in my life." That's happened to me on a few occasions. People have   come up, totally unsolicited and unexpected, and literally said words that have caused me to have tears in my eyes. They've asked if I remember them and told me I totally changed their perspective on what's important to them. Because of the influence we have— whether it's in a simple conversation, a speaking engagement, teaching a class or seminar, singing karaoke, or participating in some other avocational pursuit—it's important to remember that people are watching. It's probably easier to remember these days since so much ends up on YouTube or elsewhere online. We need to be careful, especially when we're in the public eye, to make sure that our actions mirror our intentions, and our intentions are aligned with our values. If we stay true to our core values, we can have a positive influence.

Of course the opposite is true as well. If we blow it, there are consequences. Recently, I heard a story about a famous country singer who lost his temper when he confronted an extremist group with whose message and mission he vehemently disagreed. Even though I understand the spirit of what he was saying against their inflammatory message, he did some damage to his own reputation by reacting in anger. We have to be very careful when we're in the public eye. Our influence extends beyond ourselves to the watching world.

 # Intelligence

You don't have to be a brainiac to sing karaoke, but you do need to be able to think on your feet. If I respect my audience—and respect their intelligence—I will believe that they have a baseline level of understanding, and I'll seek higher ground while I'm in front of them. I never want to take them down from where they are, but rather to lift them up. There's always someone in the room who tries to bring that level of respect and intelligence down by performing crass or stupid material. I choose to be the one who lifts them up so they don't feel the need to shower when they leave a performance just to wash off the leftover muck from the mental gutter. Be intelligent and respect others' intelligence.

 Ingredients

The ingredients to success are usually quite simple. They are practices like listening, caring, and surrounding yourself with smart people. Take these ingredients and make something meaningful with your passion and talent. Strive tirelessly to generate new valuable ideas, all the while remembering that you are doing everything for the benefit of your customer, client, spouse, friend, singing partner, KJ, or whatever "other" is in front of you. You're doing it for someone else. My performance is not for me. However, the ingredients are inside us, and it can be dangerous to neglect caring for ourselves.

There was a campaign going around that was pretty clever called I Am Second.[28] It's not, "I'm first." It's God first, me second, family and friends third. I think that's great. A lot of times, though, I struggle with the "I'm Second" idea. Sometimes I think I'm 435th or somewhere else down the line. I'm not saying my evaluation is right. There are times when I should put myself next in line behind God and my beliefs so I can make sure I'm in the best shape to serve others effectively.

It's not that you or I are in some hierarchy where if something happens to God, one of us will step in and take his place. The idea is that in order to serve others effectively, you and I need to be taking care of those things that keep us in a healthy place. You and I need to prioritize our well- being—physically, mentally, and emotionally. Thinking of ourselves with the appropriate balance of humility and respect is a crucial ingredient to delivering a strong performance that will benefit ourselves and those around us.

Integrate

We integrate our personality into every performance. We infuse our individual energies, our own sense of humor, and our unique style of presentation. Even though we may try to compartmentalize our lives into different isolated boxes, everything we do affects the other areas of our lives—our work, personality, and relationships. Whatever your vocation or avocation happen to be, it's helpful to consider the ways that these are integrated into each other and influence all other areas of life.

Try asking these questions to yourself to start you on a path of integrating positive changes into your life:

Can you think of ways to integrate fun aspects of your avocation into your work life? How might you integrate discipline and purpose into activities you do for fun?

Which strengths and ideas of others would you like to integrate into your own life?

If

Ask "What if?" It's important when you're performing someone else's music to act with that creative "if." It's thinking, "If I were them…" I've been on stage with some of the greats throughout music history, but really, they were only there in spirit. I wouldn't go so far as saying I "channel" their spirit, but I do ask imaginative questions as I approach their songs. "What would it like to be them?" or "What was it like to perform on stage in the prime of their career?"

My wife and I shared a great experience on a visit to New York City at the Waldorf Astoria Hotel. We went up to the Starlight Roof, a venue where countless legendary singers such as Frank Sinatra, Benny Goodman, Sarah Vaughn, Ella Fitzgerald, Duke Ellington—and many others—performed. We actually saw photographs on the wall of these greats making music on that stage. As I stood there in that extraordinary room and had my picture taken, I was able to spend a few moments pondering and reflecting. I thought about what it must have been like to be in the audience or even to have been one of the performers on the stage at night.

That moment stays with me. I carry it around with me when I sing karaoke or speak in front of a group. Likewise, I think, "What must it have been like to be standing beside Martin Luther King, Jr. that day when he delivered the 'I Have a Dream' speech?" and "What would it have been like to sing in front of a sold-out crowd at Carnegie Hall?"

How would it have felt to stand under the lights? What would these artists have been thinking? What kind of motivation compelled them? How full did their hearts feel? How inspired were they to give their very best show because they knew some people were there for the first and only time to hear them?"

That "if" is big.

Your Inspire Track List

1. You're the Inspiration—Chicago
2. Don't Stop Believin'—Journey
3. Imagine—The Beatles
4. Dream On—Aerosmith
5. All I Wanna Do—Sheryl Crow
6. I Believe I Can Fly—R. Kelly
7. I Get a Kick Out of You—Frank Sinatra
8. We Are Young—Fun
9. Girls Just Wanna Have Fun—Cyndi Lauper
10. We Are the Champions—Queen

What other Inspire tracks are on your list?

____

____

____

____

Rehearsal Notes

1. What are three sources of inspiration for you? Think about the people, places, books, movies, music, or avocations that energize and motivate you.

____

____

____

____

2. Ask a friend, family member, or co-worker what inspires them. As well as learning more about them, you may find a new source of inspiration for yourself in the process!

Spotlight on Kate: Office-Brightening People Person and Ballad-Singer Extraordinaire

What was your perception of karaoke before you tried it?
I thought it sounded like something fun to do occasionally. I honestly didn't know there would be people who could actually sing well, but that's what made going more enjoyable.

What linkage, if any, do you see between doing fun well and doing better work?
Excellence has always been an aspiration of mine—no matter what it is that I'm involved in—so I feel like I always want to sing the best I can when I'm there, just like I always want to give my best effort to my work during the day.

What are your "go-to" songs and why?
My favorite song to sing is "Someone to Watch Over Me" because I have always been a ballad girl. I enjoy songs that tell a story and have always preferred slower songs. To me, they are more meaningful and have more soul and heart, which is what I love in a song. I also love taking requests because I like to sing songs that my friends enjoy hearing. It makes it fun to have songs that other people want to hear you sing.

What, if anything, has karaoke taught you about yourself?
It has solidified to me that I am too hard on myself. Even with something fun and entertaining like karaoke, I have always wanted every song that I sing to sound perfect. I think it's awesome to care about doing your best, but sometimes you just have to let go of the need for everything to sound ultra-professional.

What parallels have you observed between karaoke and other areas of your life?

I have noticed that you should just have fun and not be so worried about what other people think of you. Who cares if people think you are the best singer or not? Just be you. There will always be someone more talented than you, and there will always be someone less talented than you—but none of that really matters. Whatever gifts you have been blessed with in life, you should use them to your fullest potential and enjoy life while you can because you aren't promised tomorrow. So, I think you need to just enjoy life without fear of being rejected by other people's positive or negative opinions of you. You are not defined by what you do or by how well you do it, you are defined by who you are and I think that is an important lesson to keep in mind.

What do people think about karaoke? Do you agree or disagree with their perception?

I think most people think that karaoke is a fun thing to do with your friends to celebrate a special event or to just have a night out on the town to be silly and let loose. Some people probably think that it is just a bunch of intoxicated people making fools of themselves and singing off-key. And other people look at it as a stress reliever after a long week of work where they can just go do something they enjoy with friends who enjoy the same thing. The surprising thing is that a lot of the people who go to karaoke regularly can actually sing very well. Especially living in Music City USA, there is a ton of raw talent here [in Nashville], and so when you are a musician, it's so much more fun to go when people are not only having a good time, but they actually sound good, too.

How do you incorporate fun into your life? What hobbies do you enjoy?

I have always loved singing and listening to music. I also enjoy sports and physical activities such as running, mountain biking, hiking, kayaking, swimming, boot camp,

and more. I really like being outdoors and just being active.
I also enjoy reading, watching movies and hanging out with
friends.

*What are the fun aspects of your work life? How do you pursue
loving what you do?*
  The aspect I care most about at work is making a difference
  in people's lives and spreading cheer and joy to the people
  I come in contact with on a daily basis. I believe work
  should be fun and that you should strive to be a positive,
  encouraging, and supportive addition to any team. My goal
  is to make people have a brighter day because I was a part of
  it and to make people believe in themselves. I want them to
  know not only what an asset they are to our team, but also
  that they are special and loved simply for who they are—not
  just for the job they perform.

*What do you think the karaoke experience offers people? What
does it give to you?*
  Karaoke helps people be free to be themselves. I think
  people need to let their guard down more and let themselves
  live a little. Have some fun and don't take life or yourself so
  seriously all the time. That is what it does for me. When I
  give up my fears of rejection and having to sound perfect
  or be the best all the time, life is so much more enjoyable.
  When you stop criticizing yourself and start just enjoying
  your life, you bring so much more peace and happiness not
  only to your life but to the lives of those around you. This is
  living life to the fullest and being your best self. When you
  are able to allow yourself the freedom to smile, laugh and be
  you, there is no greater gift you can give the world.

Spotlight on Gianfranco: Gourmet Chef, Food Business Promoter, and Live-Band Karaoke Enthusiast

What was your perception of karaoke before you first sang?

My first time really singing karaoke was as a college freshman in Buffalo when I was 18 with my best friend, a Korean American. We had sung in talent shows, but it was at a Chinese restaurant that had karaoke after hours, and I think my first song was Ben E. King's "Stand By Me."

I liked it. I *really* liked it. I got up and I was nervous, and I knew the song from singing it in the car. I sang it and everybody was like, "Wow!" It was immediate. I knew I was hooked. It was all about girls then and the girls liked it, so that was cool.

Do you see any linkage between doing "fun" well and doing better work?

Absolutely. When you come off the stage and you think you sounded pretty good, and everyone's clapping for you and saying, "Great job!" and you either high-five them or fist-bump them you feel amazing. You start to crave that sense of "I rocked it."

That easily applies to work. Everybody wants to be awesome at what they're doing. It's harder. It's not the same situation. You handed in a great report? Very infrequently do you get a high-five for it.

What are your go-to songs and why?

That's kind of like asking me who's my favorite kid! I guess right now my favorite song is Bruce Springsteen's "Thunder Road." It was definitely Marc Cohn's "Walking in Memphis" for a while there. Before that, probably "Turn the Page," which I still like doing, but it's such a karaoke standard that a lot of

KJs will take it off their menus because people have done it so many times. I don't mind going and having a cup of tea or a Coke, but if I'm going to have a couple of drinks, I'll do Journey or something that's harder. If everybody is bad, I'll do more adventurous stuff. If all the singers are pretty good, I'll stick with what I'm more familiar with.

Just like anything else, you gain confidence based on how you did the last time, and then you kind of warm up a little bit. You start trying different things, and your voice responds, too. I'm always cautious about what songs I choose. You want to end strong and some of the songs I choose will blow out my voice. When I do Meatloaf, I'm done. You're done after that. You're up there for seven and a half minutes just belting it out.

What, if anything, has karaoke taught you?
I'm usually a promoter, an outgoing person, but I think karaoke has made me more this way. I'm in retail sales, and I've been in retail all around food—whether for bars, restaurants, gourmet foods, supermarkets—and I've always said that if you want to hire people to sell your product, go find bartenders and servers. Good bartenders and servers are out there in front of the public the whole time and they're not afraid to approach folks and talk to people.

But the other thing after that service aspect is, I wish we could put karaoke on the interviews. You could tell a lot about a person by the songs they pick and what they perform. I'm sure there's a grad student in Sweden or somewhere doing a study on it right now—about personality types and karaoke song choices. If somebody can get up on stage, and even if they're not great, whether they're doing it silly or they're doing it serious, they get huge points with me. Maybe that's because like-to-like is a common thing, but I live for that. Then if you have somebody who can really get into a song and make the audience stop goofing around and really feel the song, that's something special.

What parallels have you observed between karaoke and other areas of your life?

When you're afraid of something, and you do it anyway, that's courage, right? No matter how many times I've done karaoke—and I must've sung at least a thousand times in front of small crowds and big crowds—there's still that little tingle of fear in my stomach. I'll give you a perfect example. Here in Portland on Monday nights, there's this place that does karaoke with a live band. The band knows 500 songs. There's no bouncing ball, there are no monitors—they just hand you the sheet music and start playing. Most of the people who get up there are pretty decent. A couple of them weren't great, but most of them were pretty decent.

I felt like it was my first time doing karaoke again. I was looking through the list, and they didn't have any of my standard, go-to songs. They had songs by artists I liked, but none of the songs that I knew really well. And without the bouncing ball or the monitor, I was scared. I was like, "I can't leave without doing a song!" And I agonized about picking one out. I finally chose Blood, Sweat, and Tears' "Spinning Wheel." It was pretty good—I liked it up there on stage with the band. You feel like a rock star! But what I remember most about that scenario was that after singing karaoke a thousand times in a bar, I felt like it was my first time. I didn't want to goof it up. There were five people in the band, and it was a real band—complete with bass guitar, electric guitar, a drummer, a keyboardist, and this one girl who was doing backup vocals and percussion. It turned out to be really awesome.

SING!

Part III:
Find Your Nexus

"Human beings can't help it: we need to belong. One of the most powerful of our survival mechanisms is to be part of a tribe, to contribute to (and take from) a group of like-minded people. We are drawn to leaders and to their ideas, and we can't resist the rush of belonging and the thrill of the new."

—*Seth Godin*[iv]

nex·us [nek-suh s] *noun*

1.a means of connection; tie; link.

2.a connected series or group.

3.the core or center, as of a matter or situation.

A nexus is what helps many of us even take the first courageous steps toward doing what we love. Belonging to a group gives us a sense of purpose greater than ourselves. It gives us energy, support, and people to share in our laughter and joy as well as our anxieties and sorrows.

Belonging to a group or community gives us a sense of identity. It helps us better understand who we are and what we want from life. And what's more—not only does a nexus help us toward our goals, it can actually dramatically improve our quality of life. Social connections reportedly alleviate stress-induced health problems and speed recovery from sickness or injury. We can also utilize our nexus as a source of encouragement—giving us the boost we need to tackle any anything and everything from sticking to a better diet and exercise plan, to making progress in personal growth and learning experiences, to pursuing a new hobby or stepping onstage at karaoke night!

Tom Kelly, co-founder of IDEO and co-author of *Creative Confidence: Unleashing the Creative Potential Within Us All* puts it this way:

> I go to Japan a lot. I started encountering karaoke about 25 years ago. And I'm thinking, why are people braver in this environment than they are back in the office? Liquid courage is part of the formula. But it's not the whole thing. Think of that karaoke room as a metaphor for your company. There are a lot of special things going on. I am going to get up there and sing a cappella in front of my friends. I'm willing to take this big risk because you're going to get up and sing next! We're all in this together. The other part is that people have turned down critical judgment, temporarily, to go into the karaoke room. The big fear holding people back from creative confidence is the fear of being judged. In the karaoke room, a colossal failure is at least as much fun as something that is really good.[v]

Psychologist James H. Fowler, who was interested in the effect of others' happiness on our own, observed that happiness reaches us through up to three degrees of connection.

And unlike other sources of happiness—like, say, material gain or an upswing in circumstances—positive relationships provide real, lasting satisfaction. Perhaps you've heard of people who return to a pessimistic mindset just a short while after winning the lottery. It's a phenomenon called "hedonic adaption," and it illustrates the truth of the old adage: Money can't buy happiness. The good news is that when we engage with a social group and develop true friendships, we are likely to continue receiving positive emotions from them—even after the "honeymoon phase" is over![vi]

> *Our happiness increases not just when our friends are happy, but when their friends and those friends' friends are happy! The effect of positive connections within a nexus is truly powerful.*

 ᴋNow Your Song

A few key things help facilitate the change from anxiety to eagerness. In karaoke performance, the first is knowing the song. The second, which is closely linked to the first, is knowing the crowd and how they will respond to your choice. Singing a song that will elicit a positive response from the audience can make all the difference in your level of confidence as you perform. Third is understanding the limitations of your own voice. If you're a baritone male, you probably aren't going to (and probably shouldn't) attempt a Whitney Houston ballad.

Those considerations are important, and many people don't think enough about them. Beyond the things within yourself that you can control, it's also important to have a supportive audience—your own group—to cheer you on. It can make a huge difference knowing that they have your back even if you mess up.

Some of the worst performances happen when the person onstage doesn't know the song very well. These are the folks who hear a song one time and think they know it. Once they get up on the stage in front of an audience and realize there's more to the song than the ten-word chorus (perhaps there's a bridge, and a couple of verses, and even a key change), they're totally lost. This doesn't just happen with notoriously long ballads like American Pie or Bohemian Rhapsody, but with many songs people attempt on a whim. The point is—Know your song. Know your voice. Know your audience.

You also want to know what you're working with. Get to know your venue. Learn what technology is available to you. In karaoke, a good sound system makes a huge difference. I love using a wireless microphone. I love a good sound system. There are certain versions of songs that sound better than others so you have to know which one is best for you. Find out if the original key fits or if you need to step it up or down. It's the same when you're in front of a group. You don't want to speak in front of a group of 2,000 people without a microphone unless you're in a room with absolutely perfect acoustics. Figure out how you can harness the available resources to help you deliver your best presentation.

Putting in a little forethought and practice can take your performance from something that intimidates or embarrasses you (and fails to impress others) to something fun and engaging for everyone.

# Never Let Them See You Sweat

When I've encountered a "first" of some kind, I've often thought back to the Rogers and Hammerstein song lyrics from the classic musical *The King and I* that Anna sings to the boy, reminding him to pretend that he's brave even when he doesn't feel like it. Projecting confidence even if I don't feel 100% secure has carried me through a number of challenging situations.

The trick is, never let them see you sweat. I learned this first as a kid when I faced my trepidation of climbing the ladder of the swimming pool high dive. You want to seem relaxed and sure of yourself even in these nerve-wracking circumstances because when you seem confident, the crowd *believes* that you're confident and responds much more positively.

In general, people don't want to hear someone who sings poorly or falls apart mid-performance. They don't want you to get up there and look stupid and waste their time and attention. The novelty of the "train wreck" performance made popular on the audition rounds of music-based reality shows wears off very quickly. What your audience really wants is for you to get up there and perform admirably and give them a reason to cheer. They want to be supportive of you because they want you to do the same for them. Often, we allow our minds to turn our allies into adversaries by thinking they wish us ill when in fact they may not even be thinking about us at all—or if they are, they actually want us to do well.

When I see someone who understands this on a karaoke stage, they put on a much better show than other singers. Building relationships with those in your nexus will help reduce "pre-show" jitters. Practicing your songs helps reinforce this. Practice can be singing in the car, in the shower, or wherever won't get you in trouble. It teaches you how to summon courage you may not already have and instills confidence in even the most insecure singer.

 # Next

On karaoke night, knowing your place in the lineup—knowing when you are "up next" is important. You don't want to miss your spot in the rotation. It's important in other areas of your life, as well. Always have in mind what's coming next. A sense of eager anticipation, engagement and excitement about family, work, and activities we love comes from the promise of what's next. None of us knows what's around the corner and that's what makes life exciting.

I hear a lot of people talk about certain events being on their "bucket list." Honestly, I have nothing for or against bucket lists. I'm bucket-list-neutral. But I don't have a bucket list. The reason is that my real life experiences have far exceeded anything that I could have imagined as a child. I would never have thought that I would travel to so many interesting places around the world. I would never have imagined having the wonderful wife, children and grandchildren I have today. I had no idea what was next. I've learned to welcome any and all new experiences that are going to be beneficial to me and those close to me, but there's no *expectation* that I'll have those exceptional moments. Nor do I expect to be disappointed if I reach the end of my days and I haven't checked off certain "bucket list" items. My whole life has been a bucket list.

The point of thinking forward to what's next isn't an attempt to exceed your own expectations. Anticipating what's next is a way of staying young. It's a way of keeping energy fresh and maintaining excitement around relationships and family. This approach is one thing I like about a particular local KJ—a gentleman named Mike. He has a great attitude, puts on a great show, and really tries to make sure the sound and staging are top-notch for the people who sing at his karaoke night each week. Mike queues up each singer's songs, and plays them in random order so that none of us knows what's going to come up next. But we do know that his tracklist is going to result in a great show. He looks around the room during certain times of the night and plans songs that will either bring the energy level up or down, or intentionally changes the atmosphere by introducing something different like country or classic rock. Mike keeps karaoke night fresh with the element of surprise.

Whether it's the invention of penicillin or Post-It notes, some of the best ideas come from unexpected sources—or even happy accidents. Surrounding ourselves with others who are curious, talented, and inspired will keep our minds fresh and optimistic by being open to future changes and continually watching for what's next.

 iNvest

Invest time and resources but do so in a strategic way. In other words, I encourage anyone who wants to be more successful tomorrow than he or she is today to first create a priority list of options and ideas that are important to customers, clients, or audience members—and then invest primarily in those things.

Invest in what you know will lead you from a familiar place of comfort and enjoyment to a more challenging, productive arena. It's not wise for people to totally reinvent themselves if it means completely moving away from what's gotten them to where they are today. The goal is to make informed investments that move you the right distance in the right direction.

Traditional consumer marketing that relies on television, radio, and print buys is being turned on its head by new internet and event-based interactions with the customer. Innovative marketers continue to find new approaches to grab the customer's attention in order to convince them to buy the product, subscribe to the service, or engage in the experience they're staging.

You yourself are the best investment and the most effective marketing. Joe Pine and Jim Gilmore, authors of *The Experience Economy,* describe how marketing is secondary to the experience. They quote legendary business consultant Peter Drucker, who once said that "the aim of marketing is to make selling superfluous." Pine and Gilmore take that statement further to contend that the role of "placemaking"— or providing an authentic experience for your customers—is to render marketing superfluous.[29] We must create and stage great experiences for our customers. In essence, the experience is the marketing. Whether our customers are people buying coffee or piano lessons or heavy equipment or our advice— creating a great experience for them ensures that we're going to become their number one provider of choice for that good, service, or experience.

In order to become that preferred person or company, we must invest in our own education, enlightenment, and pursuits—whether vocational or avocational—that create energy within us and keep us looking for what's next. Investing in ourselves will keep us fresh and relevant to those around us.

Investment also keeps us out of harm's way when things don't go as we had hoped. Failure to plan for a rainy day usually means that when the rain comes, you're going to be soaked to the skin. Our 35th U.S. president, John F. Kennedy, famously stated that, "The time to repair the roof is when the sun is shining."[30] Thinking ahead and investing is essential to long-term success and growth. We invest in intellectual capital the same way we do in the financial marketplace. In either case, you can't invest after the fact. It would be like going to the cashier window at the horserace track and saying, "I want to place a bet on the winner of the last race." It doesn't work. Invest wisely beforehand.

 # Now

Don't delay. It's time. The great clock on the wall says "Now." There is no better time to begin the process of investing in yourself, others around you, your business, and your nexus than right now. Procrastination shouldn't be a profession.

I like the writings and witty quotations of Mark Twain, so my apologies for the following criticism. He said, "Never put off till tomorrow what you can do day after tomorrow just as well."[31] While I laugh at the sentiment behind the quote,

I certainly don't agree with it. I believe you should never put off till tomorrow what you can do right now. If you've turned your preparations into procrastinations, start now. If you've delayed for longer than necessary without a good reason, start now. You never want to start a song late. You never want to show up to a meeting late.

We've all done it. But today is a new day and opportunity so start now. There's power in now.

 # New

"New" is an interesting concept. What is new to some people may be passé or old to others. "New" is a state of mind and a state of current business. Even old things can become new. I believe in recycling, both in a literal sense of being a responsible steward of the earth's resources and in the recycling of business ideas and concepts. What might appear new on the scene might be just a tweaking or recycling of an existing concept. The ability to refresh and repackage the world around us gives us limitless access to what is "new." We can appreciate anything and everything all over again.

It certainly happens in music. How many songs, movies, or books are really just recycling of concepts that have been shared with audiences for years or decades or even centuries? You can see this when you look at some of the modern film adaptations of Shakespeare's work. The source material is several centuries old, yet the stories are regarded as new when they hit the silver screen.

It's the same way with music. If you take an unplugged version of a hard rock song, or sample a ballad and put it in a rap song, people will consider the final product a new work of art even though it may just be recycled from the work of another artist.

"New" is a concept that we should constantly seek. Appreciating what's new will keep our minds fresh and our creativity honed to a very sharp edge. If we keep our eyes and ears open to the new, we can become better and better at what we do, how we serve our customers, and how we relate to others on a personal level. Frequently ask these questions of yourself—Have I made any new friends lately? Have I learned anything new lately? Have I joined a new nexus lately?

Sometimes, when you hear about what's new, people will throw out the word "nouveau." The label "nouveau" indicates something new and trendy and largely untried. I'm always a little cautious when I hear this term used to describe something that's just arrived on the scene. In the music world, I'm never quite sure how much staying power nouveau ideas, songs, and artists will have. The positive side of this label is that if you're considered nouveau, you're not stale. You're not locked into a conventional way of thinking. You're open to new, exciting, different ideas. The negative side is that you could just be a flash in the pan. You could have an idea that is popular today and gone tomorrow. As many hit-makers know, nouveau can be a one-hit wonder. The hit itself is fantastic, but finding out what has staying power is even better.

 ## iNnovate

Gerald Haman is the founder of SolutionPeople, an innovation and creativity firm in Chicago—and is also an avid karaoke enthusiast.

In his advanced innovation workshop, Gerald explains that the difference between creativity and innovation is that innovation is "the ability to take creative ideas and make money doing them." To innovate is to invent new opportunities to creatively express yourself or share value in your personal life or business. It's great to innovate in music as well. Some of the great musicians of the 20th century were innovators. Sean Combs (known by a variety of aliases such Puff Daddy, P. Diddy, and so on) was a middle-class kid who grew up to become a world-famous hip hop star and multi-millionaire businessman. Jay-Z transformed himself from growing up in poverty to being a performer, multi-industry mogul, and even part owner of the Brooklyn Nets. Innovation isn't determined by your background, your education, or your level of skill. It's about your willingness to look outside of your ordinary circumstances to what could be and then to work hard enough and smart enough to bring about what you want to exist in the world.

 # Never Give Up

Life is challenging. Sometimes it's tempting to throw our hands up and say, "I just can't do this another day." Yet if the course of history had taught us anything, it is that it's important to never give up. We need to face our challenges and say, "I know that if I stay the course, reach out to those around me, and utilize my God-given strengths, I can keep on going."

This type of dogged tenacity is the basis of a famous quote by British prime minister Winston Churchill. He visited a school just a year after the bombings and air-raids of World War II. Praising Britain's steadfastness against the tyranny of Nazi

Germany, he urged the school boys to "never give in, never give in, never, never, never—in nothing, great or small, large or petty—never give in except to convictions of honour and good sense. Never yield to force; never yield to the apparently overwhelming might of the enemy."[32] That's a great lesson in military strategy as well as in life. Never give in, never give up.

When the going gets tough—and you're tempted to give up—turn to your nexus. They are your best source of encouragement and support in times like these.

 # Near

What is near and dear to you? It's a great concept to keep in mind when you're working, spending time with loved ones, or pursuing your avocation. You want to make sure you keep your loved ones nearby. It's always thrilling when we see our dreams and aspirations, whether they are personal or professional goals, drawing nearer to us. It's part of that wonderful emotion called anticipation. There's a reason we use the expression "near and dear." When something is drawing nearer to us, it takes shape and becomes real. We can almost see and hear and smell it, and we believe that it is tangible at last. It's an incredible joy to experience your desires drawing near to you. Anticipation makes the act of reaching out and taking hold of what we want that much more rewarding. We want to draw nearer to what we love so our dreams will draw near to us.

Who are the people near you who encourage you and inspire you to be your best?

Who are the nearby people you seek to inspire and bring into your nexus community?

 # Neighborhood

It's another way of saying "community" or giving specific geography to your nexus. Being a part of a neighborhood means that there are people nearby who notice when you're not around. These are the people who miss you when you're away. Accountability goes hand-in-hand with neighborhood. The same people who know when you're there and miss you when you're not also hold you accountable for your behavior, and you do the same for them. If I see someone acting in a way that is detrimental to themselves or those around them, I will let them know. Not because I'm an authority, but because I care about them and about the well-being of the neighborhood.

Knowing those around you means taking the time to understand what's important to them and what they enjoy and expect from the time you spend together. That's a crucial part of what makes you a neighbor. Showing that you are a caring person who understands what they want and need benefits the entire neighborhood. A neighborhood where you feel comfortable and at home is a safe place to be honest and emotionally vulnerable with others.

I enjoy being a part of the neighborhood at karaoke nights in the Nashville area. I also enjoy being welcomed as a visitor and visiting performer at other people's karaoke night neighborhood. It is a great experience which stretches me and helps me learn about people. I believe that it helps make me a better teacher, husband, father and friend. I know for certain that I have empathy and respect for people of different backgrounds and beliefs as a result of visiting their neighborhoods on karaoke night.

 ıNformed

Abraham Lincoln once said that if he had eight hours to cut down a tree, he would take six hours to sharpen the axe.[33] Lumberjack techniques aside, the point is that preparation is essential to success. Study every aspect of your pursuit, whether diving into the details of a hobby, researching information for a meeting, or learning a new academic subject.

You can't speak with any real authority off the top of your head. Everyone is guilty of speaking without thinking on occasion, but it can kill your credibility to spout off about unfounded opinions or assumptions. If we want to deliver something that matters to people, we must spend time gaining knowledge to really understand the subject. Invest the time needed to learn about a subject before speaking profusely about it.

Our best performances come from our best preparation.

In his autobiography *Surprised By Joy,* C.S. Lewis relates a particular conversation he had as a boy in grade school (or primary school, as they call it in Great Britain) with a professor. They were walking across the campus and the professor asked him a question. Lewis gave his ready response, to which the professor retorted, "Oh really? And why do you think that?" Lewis stammered and stuttered and had no real answer. He had not really studied the subject of which he spoke so quickly and confidently and he had no real basis for his opinion. He was basically just shooting off at the mouth. He made up for it later with years of scholarship, of course, but it was a great lesson for him at that young and impressionable age—

never speak out of ignorance. Often people will make a statement as if it's an absolute, irrefutable fact but when asked why, they simply shrug and say, "Well, that's just how I feel." There might be six or seven billion feelings to the contrary to that opinion around the world. Who knows? Are any of our thoughts and feelings rooted in reality? Are they grounded in substantive beliefs that lead us to feel confident that there's truth behind what we're saying? The more informed we become, the stronger our foundation for what we think, say and do becomes. From this strong foundation we can better develop our nexus and make helpful and meaningful connections with others.

Our nexus itself is a tremendous resource of information. Want to be better informed about music, life, and other topics? Engage your nexus and learn from the informed people around you.

 eNvision

A goal is a dream with a deadline. —Napoleon Hill[34]

In the words of Jesse Jackson, "If my mind can conceive it, and my heart can believe it, I know I can achieve it."[35] We have to envision our goals for all the different areas of life. There's a book that many business leaders have read called *Think and Grow Rich* by Napoleon Hill. Reportedly, Andrew Carnegie, John D. Rockefeller, Cornelius Vanderbilt, and a number of great business leaders and industrial magnates from the early 1900s read this book and applied its principles. The essence of the book is that if you want to succeed in an area of life you must first want that success more than anything else. You must speak verbally what those goals are on a daily basis—he says morning and night, but at least twice a day—and actually say aloud what you want. In doing that, he says, you will envision what your goals are.

I believe that in preparing for a great stage performance or an effective business presentation, the same rules apply. We must understand what we hope to accomplish and then tell ourselves, even verbally, what we want the outcome to be. We have to give ourselves a definite timeline and hold ourselves accountable. This way, our goal becomes more than just a hopeful thought or a fleeting idea that passes by. We have to tell ourselves that this is something we're capable of achieving. A positive affirmation or pick-me-up mantra may be good enough to help get us started but it's really not enough to enable us to follow through. We must ask ourselves, "Have I studied hard enough? Have I gained knowledge? Do I apply knowledge effectively? Am I surrounding myself with a nexus of people who are supportive and skilled, talented and willing?" These questions and statements are essential to envisioning our goals.

We hear ambitious and creative people repeat the same question, "What will my life look like at the next level?" This question has motivated performers who, even when they were sleeping in cars or slumming it in flea-bag apartments, used it to fuel their desire to press forward. When they finally achieve a high level of success they say, "I'm not surprised. I knew I was going to arrive here because I was committed." Obviously, they were envisioning the success quite clearly before they attained it.

We can't control catastrophes or unforeseen setbacks but we can play a part in the way the future unfolds in how we approach possibility.

Envisioning is vital to a successful approach and it is the opposite of intellectual laziness. Giving in to intellectual laziness is when we say, "I'm just going to walk along, not really do anything out of the ordinary, and just kind of get by." It's a fine mindset perhaps, for those who have no real ambition, and it's where many people live every day. In fact, it's where most people are satisfied to live until the day the light bulb clicks and they realize what could have been. Suddenly, the "just get by" folks wish they'd done things differently. Changing your life begins with envisioning the possibilities. Then can you start to channel your preparations, energies, and efforts toward what truly matters to you.

 iNsight

____

It always seems much easier to have insight into other people than into myself. Why is that? It's because I, just like everyone else, am tempted to perceive myself as the person I want to be rather than what I really am—a person with weaknesses, flaws, and occasional blind-spots. Nevertheless, I hope to continue to develop more honest insight into who I really am. One cautionary note about insight: Always examine yourself first and more closely than others. We can't control what others do. We can only control *our own* behavior. Having insight into ourselves is therefore a much more helpful starting point than ignoring ourselves in hopes of figuring out   everyone else around us.

Insight is necessary to understanding our competition. If anybody is still alive, active, and earning money for what they do, they're doing something right. Otherwise they wouldn't be around for you to notice. They are in some way, appealing to a particular audience. If I want to grow my business it serves me well to understand what they do and how they do it. If I stand back and throw rocks over the fence at them and say, "You're no good! I don't like you!" like some petulant kid or bury my head in the sand and pretend that what they're doing is not successful, I'm deluding myself. Yet if I look at their success and say, "You know what? They're doing something that has an impact—I'm going to write some things down," I am in a better position. I can take note of what I like or dislike that they're doing.

Maybe a third column will emerge of any things I don't really understand.

With this list of new insights in hand, I can better understand my competition. Perhaps I can pick up a couple of tips. If they are doing things I dislike, I can review the list and find out what their customers appreciate and why. If they're doing something I don't understand, I can research and ask customers, "What if we did that?" This is practice is a powerful way to gain insight.

In karaoke, insight helps us recognize the value of other people's performances. As with improvisation, insight is about being additive rather than subtractive—building up rather than tearing down. It's achieved with an attitude of "yes, and" instead of "no way, that won't work."

Disney has an extraordinary insight into what their customer wants. They understand that they don't compete just with Universal Studios or Six Flags Amusement Parks. They don't compete just with other movies and television shows. Their competition is *everybody else who gets money for goods, services or experiences.* They look at the ways other industries do business and take cues that can help them become a better business operator. It's a phenomenally wise way to gain insight. When I look at what other people are willing to spend their money on, I may discover the seed for a new business opportunity. The more insight I gain, the more possibilities I uncover.

 # iNtuition

It's not magical—it's a knack for reading situations and people. It's the ability to see a little farther down the road to whatever is coming our way. Intuition is often the result of careful observation of people in situations over a number of years. Some are intuitive from a young age but for most people intuition develops more fully at middle age when they've had plenty of life experiences and encountered a variety of people.

Sometimes people describe their intuition as "just having a feeling." Perhaps they feel that something's not right or they develop a sense of unease when walking down a dark alley. It enables us to make a decision without consciously going through a list of items and checking them off. It's being sensitive to people and to what's happening below the surface.

The more we develop our intuition, the easier it becomes for us resist stereotyping other people. What happens is that in the process of opening myself up and getting to know them better, something changes. I start trying to understand them and learn what motivates them. I find out what things they know that I don't and what beneficial connections they possess. Some of my closest relationships and most valuable business has come from people who on first impression, I walked away from with a less-than-perfect feeling. It's not always kismet. We don't always hit it off with people right away. Sometimes you have to wade into the process a bit before you gain enough understanding to bridge the gap. Developing intuition takes time but is worth the investment. Intuitive people are others-focused. When you walk into a room, intuition isn't jumping to the question, "Well, what are they thinking about me?" Instead, intuition is wondering what others are thinking, what's going on behind the scenes and how you can make someone's day better by recognizing the under-the-surface realities that matter to them. An intuitive person who has worked hard to develop this insight can read people and understand when they're at the end of their patience. Intuition can alert you when you're at risk of overplaying your hand. What might seem funny to you might wear out your welcome if you don't listen to your intuition. Likewise, if you're on the stage performing a song that no one in that group has heard, it's going to fall on unappreciative ears and people will wonder why you're there. Developing your intuition—and listening to it—enables you to consistently connect with your audience.

Intuition is not something supernatural or spiritual. It's an amalgamation of life experiences and conversations that take place over a long period of time. It's similar to the ability that Malcolm Gladwell described in his book *Blink* of making a decision without putting a great deal of thought into it.[36] Intuition just comes to you because there's a convergence of life experience along with everything else you've learned and dreamed—and you have a sense about things.

When we listen to it on a regular basis, intuition leads us to insight. Business guru Tom Peters once had his work described as "a blinding flash of the obvious."[37] Insight is the same. It's the sum total of our powers of observation, our intelligence, our openness, and our ability to articulate it all in a meaningful way. We gain it through the process of asking questions and trusting others. We become insightful as we acquire more life experience and keep the little child inside each of us alive. Maintaining a vibrant sense of curiosity is essential to increasing our insight into any situation. Continue to have a desire to know and grow.

 # Nerd

The word "nerd" refers to anyone who has an obsession with knowledge in a particular area—someone who loves learning just for the sake of over-learning and willingly receives good-natured verbal abuse from others for it. It's good to be a nerd about some things. Diving headlong into an area of interest can be rewarding and energizing.

Nerds are vital members of their nexus communities. When a member of a group develops deep knowledge about a shared area of interest—and can share what he or she has learned with others—everyone within the nexus benefits. A nexus is at its most powerful anytime a "nerd" joins forces with practical, action-oriented group members. Like a show-stopping duet, the collaboration is greater than anything the individual nexus members could contribute on their own.

# Narrow

No one is an expert on everything. Another appropriately humbling way to say it is that everyone is stupid about something. Narrowing your focus is vital to achieving a high level of performance. This is true in relationships, work, vocations, or avocations.

Once in a while a person is called a "jack of all trades." When you take that colloquialism and apply it to real life, it means, "I know a little about a lot of things, but not much about anything in particular." A person like that, while they may make for interesting dinner conversation, is less likely to succeed because they don't specialize in any specific area. It's great to freely explore a broad range of hobbies, writing, and conversations. At the same time there are moments that require us to narrow our focus and get stuff done. This strategy leads to increased insight and expertise in your work life. Narrowing your focus goes hand-in-hand with Napoleon Hill's advice to first envision whatever it is you want to achieve. Narrow your focus to your most important goals.

Your senses are often the best guide to beginning to narrow your focus. Our company's EatnLearn journeys, which consist of immersive food and beverage sampling and education, are truly what you would call sensory excursions. A common part of these journeys is an exercise where we send groups of two or three people out together into the marketplace. Their challenge is to look at a certain display in a store, restaurant, or sidewalk café and describe it using only the narrowed down sensory criteria of sight and smell, taste and touch, or sight and sound. We want them to narrow their scope so that they can really understand some of the key elements of the restaurant, shop, bistro, or retail store. Getting in touch with your senses creates an extraordinary experience of a business. You begin to see that business through a fresh, new lens. Narrowing focus enriches your entire perspective.

On the karaoke stage, at a business meeting, or when attempting a new avocation on the weekend, we can all benefit from narrowing our focus to those strengths we know we possess and to areas in which we truly shine. It's not an excuse to only do the familiar, easy things. Rather, we take on new challenges without trying to do everything at once or on our own. A narrow focus gives us the power of sharp senses and keeps our attention on the essentials.

 # Name

Motivational speaker and writer Dale Carnegie once said that "a person's name is to that person the sweetest and most important sound in any language."[39]

I've found that in my favorite avocational pursuit—karaoke—having a stage name is very useful. When I first started performing, I didn't want to be singled out and identified by my actual name. Instead, I intentionally crafted a stage persona which I continue to use today, a little over twenty years later. I do this for a couple of key reasons. First, I want people to recognize and appreciate the persona that I've created in that particular setting apart from who I am outside of that setting.

Secondly, I want to break down whatever barriers, real or imagined, that might exist between myself and others—

differences in education, career, socioeconomic status, neighborhood, and so on. When we show up for karaoke night we're all there for a common purpose and that is to spend time together and to perform.

Using my real name and sharing details of the rest of my life outside of the karaoke setting can detract from the experience. It can distract me and limit my ability to enjoy being in the moment for an hour or two while we're performing. That's why I choose to use a different name when performing onstage. It has nothing to do with denying the rest of my life or creating an alternate reality. It's about adapting to that particular situation, building an experience, and contributing to the quality of the show.

So how can each of us create a persona—or name— for ourselves? Whether at work or play, consistency and excellence go the furthest in making a name for yourself. Honesty, integrity, and concern for others and their success all contribute to the process as well. Taking on a new name happens by adopting the principle from improvisational theatre that it's always better to be additive and encouraging to the other person rather than detracting and saying no. It's always "yes-and"—encouraging that person by building upon their story. Crafting a persona and making a name for yourself happen best within a thriving nexus, promoting a culture of mutual respect and contributing to one another's success.

Natural

Sometimes you hear of someone referred to as "a natural." Perhaps they're exceptionally talented in a certain area without having to try very hard at it. The problem for most of us? It's pretty rare to succeed at something without a lot of hard work. Our natural starting point is nowhere near expertise. Once in a while, we are fortunate to discover something that we feel we were born to do. We all have untested natural talents and abilities that—with hard work and perseverance—we can develop into something extraordinary. Your nexus can help you discover what your natural giftings are, what your natural environment is, and what the natural next steps are for you.

What individuals or groups of people do you feel are a natural fit for you socially and professionally?

Is there something you're always been interested in learning about or doing—to the point that you'd say you have a "natural bent" toward it?

How can you develop your natural strengths and talents instead of fighting the tide of what feels unnatural, artificial, or forced for you?

Normal

Let's imagine we were to plot a particular moment in time on a map. Five years later, we look at the map again and come back to visit that same place. We might be surprised at how many changes have occurred in that location over the time we were away. If, however, we marked that particular place in time on our map but continued to visit that same location day in and day out over the five years, we may not be aware of the changes that were gradually taking place. Over that entire span of time we would, in fact, be adapting to the new normal.

Our lives and the world around us are constantly changing—sometimes slowly, sometimes at a break-neck rate of speed. It's important to keep track of our own pace and where we are in relation to our goals. We may have personal goals to fix up our home or lose weight or become more wealthy or educated. Keeping track of these specific targets over time helps us not fall prey to slow, unnoticeable adaptation to the new normal. You've probably heard the analogy of the frog in boiling water. A frog will jump out of water that's already boiling but it will gradually adjust to the temperature if it's heated slowly enough (by the way, you're welcome for the culinary tip if you were looking for free frog-cooking advice!).

It's the same reality in our lives. We can allow time to pass without really noticing it and without having any meaningful insight about what's actually happening. Because our "normal" changes so gradually, we're not keenly aware of where we hope to go. Keeping a personal diary or journal, setting aside time to review progress periodically, and asking others to hold us accountable are all effective means to help us avoid slipping into a slowly boiling "new normal."

Just like you don't want to get distracted and miss you cue while singing karaoke, you also want to stay aware and vigilant for opportunities and important moments. Check in with yourself often to make sure "normal" life isn't actually the extraordinary passing you by!

# Network

Networking with your audience is a key to successful performances. Pay attention to who was just onstage and who is coming up next so you contribute to a successful show. Even performers who are known for their outrageous antics do so because they know it's what the audience expects. Get to know the crowd—their likes and dislikes—and seek to deliver what they will enjoy and appreciate. This engagement can start with simply striking up a conversation with the fellow performers around you. Ask questions, such as, "What is your favorite karaoke song?" or "Who is your go-to artist?" There are plenty of conversation starters you can use. Networking allows you to gather insight to help you create a "wow" performance.

Who is your audience? What do they expect from you?

Who has gone before you and how can you learn from or build upon their example? Does your presentation enrich and add to the audience's experience or does it detract from their enjoyment?

# Night Vision

Night vision is the ability to see what others cannot. We practice looking into what is dark and obscure to find possibility and inspiration. In so doing we learn to perform at a level that exceeds people's expectations.

Everyone makes presumptions about others at first glance—it's an unavoidable human impulse. When someone else sees you in a certain way based on your age, height, weight, or ethnicity—they often make assumptions about you as an individual. It's not always malicious. Sometimes it's entirely unconscious but it still happens whether the assessment is fair and accurate or not.

When you have night vision you begin to see beyond the obvious and notice the fine details others might miss. Specific details about dress and posture, song selection, expression and attitude, food or beverage preferences, the way people interact and socialize—all these bits of information can teach us more than we realize.

Night vision—looking into the darkness of the unknown—is very valuable in business as well as in stage performance. By putting on these metaphorical "night-vision goggles" we achieve a level of success that other people can't simply because they don't have the skill and perspective—or "sight"— *You can learn infinitely more about people when you not only take in the surface information, but also explore who they are beyond what is easy to see at first glance.* that we do. Night vision is a skill you must cultivate over time and with a great deal of patience. It is an extraordinary asset in understanding the people and possibilities around you.

kNock-Out

One of the most exciting moments for fans of professional boxing is the knockout. Likewise, when a performance is incredibly memorable, deeply meaningful, or approaches the level of life-changing, we might refer to it as a "knockout" performance. Why is that? It's because the performance managed to move us from one state of consciousness to another, just like a knockout punch by a professional fighter.

A knockout performance by a professional businessperson or an avid stage performer is one that has lasting impact on the audience (your nexus) as well as a lasting impact on the performer. A knockout performance will dramatically boost your onstage confidence. Once you achieve a higher level of excellence than ever before, nothing less can ever fill that creative void. It's Luciano Pavoratti or Marianne Anderson delivering a soaring aria in an opera, or Sarah Vaughn covering five octaves in a jazz number, Mariah Carey hitting an impossibly high note on the proper pitch, or rumbling a very low note like the Oak Ridge Boys. These are once-in-a-lifetime heights and depths that define a knockout performance.

Whitney Houston gave a knockout performance in her legendry rendition of the "Star Spangled Banner." The knockout starts at that penultimate moment when you know you're going to see an incredible performance. You know as soon as it happens that you've witnessed something extraordinary.

 # Nerve

There's a reason so many people have stage fright. It takes a lot of nerve to be vulnerable. It takes a lot of nerve to step up. Throughout life there are opportunities to shrink back or to boldly go forward. Steely determination, guts, bravado, brassiness—whatever you want to call it—speaks volumes about you. Nerve says, "I have decided this is the route I'm taking and I will go for it." You may be wondering—if nerve is so important, how do we get our hands on it? It all comes down to a conscious decision. It's refusing any other path besides the one that leads you forward.

Ulysses S. Grant once said that much of his success as a general wasn't due to the fact that he was a better strategist—it was due to his refusal to go backward—he simply refused to retreat. He continued to go forward no matter what.[40] In so doing the Union forces were victorious in the Civil War. Another example of nerve at work is the truism that the people who ask are the people who get. It's very difficult for the average non-superhero to read someone's mind. If a person doesn't have the nerve to step forward and outright say what they want to do like, "I would like to do _____" or "I would like you to help me with _____," then it's not likely that anyone will really know what they want. If you don't have the nerve to boldly state your purpose or ask for what you want, you probably won't get the desired results.

Getting on stage takes that kind of nerve. Like most personality traits or behaviors that have both a positive and negative side to them, nerve is not always pleasant. Being bold can also be brash and brashness is boldness that is not under control. When we went cliff jumping at Rock Island State Park, leaping off that 30-foot bluff into murky water took some nerve—or possibly stupidity. After having done it once it didn't require that same level of nerve and after the third time it really didn't require nerve at all.

You can learn infinitely more about people when you not only take in the surface information, but also explore who they are beyond what is easy to see at first glance.

Nimble

Have you had to jump over any candlesticks lately? Sometimes in life we get so busy that we can feel the heat creeping a little too close for comfort. That's why it's vital to stay nimble.

Whenever you're reading an audience from the stage or working alongside others in a business setting, being able to change directions on a dime is crucial. The ability to read your audience or coworkers and make adjustments to your presentations show that you are nimble. You are able to remain professional while changing certain components of your onstage performance or your business presentations. Being nimble means always listening with your whole self to recognize how your audience is responding to you. Nimble people make changes on the fly when we sense that we are not connecting with the audience.

Break routine and do things differently once in a while. Avoid boring yourself and others by singing the same songs the same way night after night. Take on new challenges and stretch yourself. Do the same in relationships or business. This way you won't be afraid to go out and try something new. In our conversations about work and life, my wife and I frequently reference a Ray Bradbury quote, "You've got to jump off cliffs all the time and build your wings on the way down."[41]

In the face of many challenges, this serves us well. If you are willing to take risks and try something new, you may fail. But within that failure is the kernel for your future success.

It may feel safe to do the same routine over and over again, but it's boring and limiting. New ideas seldom spring out of the same monotonous activity. We must be willing to step back and look at things differently. There are very simple and practical ways to break out of the rut of ordinary thinking. Oftentimes when I'm facilitating a training session that lasts for several hours I'll ask everyone during a break to pick up all their books, laptops, and everything else and move to another place in the room. This change provides each person with a fresh perspective and inspires them to generate new ideas.

We can get locked into a certain way of seeing life but once we move around, everything changes. It's amazing how a little movement or shift in perspective can change our way of thinking and aid our creativity.

At times you may want to change midstream to wake up the audience. Or you may want to shift your emphasis in order to make a vital connection with a fellow business person. You've got to stay quick and nimble. You've gotta jump over those candlesticks just like Jack.

kNock on Doors

Continue to seek opportunities to engage your nexus. Pursuing their time and attention takes tremendous nerve and the willingness to never give up. After you've taken time to do the heavy lifting of research and begun to try out some new ideas it's time to knock on doors. Knocking on doors means that you're not willing to settle for the status quo. Instead you say to yourself, "What *else* is there that I could do?"

When I visit a new city I love to put "knocking on doors" into practice by finding unfamiliar karaoke venues to perform in. I have discovered many new favorite stages and new karaoke-enthusiast friends in the process!

Looking for new and different opportunities keeps you from settling into a mode of complacency and resignation to the way things are or always have been. Constantly referring back to the way things were in years past is not a productive practice whether in business or performance. Learning from past experiences can be most beneficial when they help us frame up our plans for moving forward. Don't let yourself become discouraged or bogged down by the past. The whole point of knocking on doors is for the doors to open so we can step over the threshold.

What doors that seem shut could you knock on?

What discouraging experiences could you draw lessons from instead of feeling defeated by a shut door?

 # Number One Hit

Everybody has a favorite song. Every musician dreams of having a number-one hit. The truth is there's no single, definitive number-one hit if you are part of a thriving nexus.

There will be an equal number of different number-one hits, each held in the minds of those individuals. As a performer, your role is to connect with your audience in a meaningful way in the brief time you have the stage. You want to bring familiarity and fun into the moment. On karaoke night you want to give them a reason to cheer you on, to get up and dance, or to sing along with you. In this way each listener feels like they can relate to you. They believe that you understand who they are and what is important to them. Who knows? They just may tweak their own list of favorites to include you in the top ten.

 Nobody to Somebody

Dean Martin had a great song about the importance of others' care for you and how it can change your whole identity. Finding purpose in life through faith, family, or a meaningful endeavor whether it's work or avocation, can instill a sense of somebody-ness into everybody.

I have a saying that I particularly like to use: Everybody is "extraordinarily ordinary." By that I mean that everyone has extraordinary talents and insight.

Everybody has incredible stories to tell. Everybody has extraordinary qualities all wrapped up in an ordinary appearance. If you walk through a crowded shopping mall, airport, bus terminal, or down a busy sidewalk, you'll see tens and hundreds and thousands of ordinary-looking people. Each person has extraordinary things to share if only given the opportunity. Moving from nobody to somebody? Everybody's there if we look close enough. All it takes is finding a stage to unleash that extraordinary somebody for others to recognize and enjoy.

 ᴇNthusiasm

Ralph Waldo Emerson once said, "Nothing great is ever achieved without enthusiasm."[42] He was right about that. Enthusiasm is an emotion closely related to optimism. As long as we're enthusiastic, optimistic, and excited about what we're doing, that contagion spreads to other people. It encourages them to embrace enthusiasm and to immerse themselves in it. Enthusiasm is beneficial when we perform onstage, engage with customers and clients, or spend time with loved ones.

Former U.S. Secretary of State Colin Powell claimed that "perpetual optimism is a force multiplier."[43] As a high-ranking career military officer, Powell used a military analogy to describe the tremendous impact of optimism. When you have soldiers on the ground, you have a certain sized force— let's say a force of a thousand. When you put guns in the hands of those soldiers, the weapons act as force multipliers. If you bring in tanks for soldiers to drive they become an even more significant force multiplier by increasing the impact of the soldiers with weapons.

You can multiply the force exponentially depending on what kind of tools or enablers you put in place. For the benefit of us civilians Powell described optimism as a powerful force multiplier the same way he would tanks or planes. Optimism within yourself or your organization is a significant force multiplier. You can achieve more from your nexus if everyone is optimistic about the outcome.

As a speaker, presenter, and performer, your energy and enthusiasm can affect the entire audience. If your energy is lagging, your performance can be very passé, easily forgettable, and boring. Yet if you bring energy and enthusiasm to the stage, you're properly prepared, and you give your best to your audience, you're almost certain to be a rousing success. People remember your enthusiasm. Late Apple CEO Steve Jobs mastered the art of sharing his enthusiasm to others to the point that they became enthusiastic, too. He practiced for hours and hours in advance of every presentation in order to powerfully communicate his message with passion and enthusiasm.

Ask yourself—Am I a fan of what I'm doing? Am I prepared? Am I giving my very best? My audience will know if I'm not fully engaged, if I haven't invested enough preparation time, or if I'm not giving it my all. Sincere, heartfelt, impassioned enthusiasm is what the audience will remember.

Your Nexus Track List:

1.   You're Nobody Till Somebody Loves You—Dean Martin
2.   I Wanna Dance With Somebody—Whitney Houston
3.   Let's Stay Together—Al Green
4.   Come Together—The Beatles
5.   We Built This City—Starship
6.   Friends in Low Places—Garth Brooks
7.   One—U2
8.   Lean On Me—Bill Withers
9.   Natural Woman—Aretha Franklin
10. Your Song—Elton John

What other Nexus tracks are on your list?

____

____

____

____

Rehearsal Notes

1. What interests, talents, and strengths do you have?

____

____

____

____

2. Are you a part of a nexus involving those interests, talents, and strengths? If not, how might you be able to connect with people in your nexus over the next 90 days? What strategies will you use to make this happen?

Spotlight on Jillene: Dancer Turned Singer-Songwriter and Karaoke Aficionado

What was your perception of karaoke before you tried it?
I thought it looked fun. I was always a dancer, never a singer —I was too afraid to sing.

What linkage, if any, do you see between doing fun well and doing better work?
My work is fun, so I don't feel I have to sacrifice fun to do a good job.

What are your "go-to" songs and why?
"Here for the Party" by Gretchen Wilson, "Pour Me" by Trick Pony, "What's Up?" by 4 Non Blondes, "Heartbreaker" by Pat Benatar, and "Any Way You Want It" by Journey. They are crowd-pleasers and high-energy songs that are also fun to sing.

What, if anything, has karaoke taught you about yourself?
It's taught me that I should just go for it sometimes—and not be shy. I won't sing a song unless I know it. It has given me confidence.

What parallels have you observed between karaoke and other areas of your life?
It helped me to be more comfortable with the band I was with. I was able to learn singing and performing. It was a gateway for getting into writing music and performing music, not just dancing.

What do people think about karaoke? Do you agree or disagree with their perception?

People who are not involved with karaoke look at it like it is kind of a joke. They assume that all karaoke singers are terrible singers—until they see an actual show. Then they realize that there are some really good singers at karaoke night! I disagree with the negative view and try to promote the positive view.

How do you incorporate fun into your life? What hobbies do you enjoy?

I enjoy entertaining and throwing parties. Another one of my hobbies is making and selling art. I like to walk, spend time outdoors, yoga, dance—and my number one hobby is of course, singing.

What are the fun aspects of your work life? How do you pursue loving what you do?

It's about the art. I am very lucky and blessed that I can pursue a singing and songwriting career. I am able to work part-time and pursue my hobbies which sometimes include a financial element as well.

What do you think the karaoke experience offers people? What does it give to you?

It offers people an opportunity to come out of their shell a little. People who are seemingly too shy will get up onstage and get hooked on the feeling of being in the spotlight. It gives people a different outlook. People who don't want to pursue a career in entertainment get a chance to shine for a night.

Spotlight on Mark:
A Realtor with a Passion
for Music and Good Times
with Friends

What was perception of karaoke before you tried it?
I didn't know much about it, so I didn't really know what to expect.

Tell us about your first time singing. Who got you into karaoke?
I sang probably 20 years ago in a small bar in Nashville one night. A friend of a friend took me there rather spontaneously.

What linkage do you see between doing fun well and doing better work?
If something's worth doing, it's worth doing well—seems applicable to everything in life.

What are your "go-to" songs and why?
"Pretty Woman" by Roy Orbison, "Jack & Diane" by John Mellencamp, and "Walking in Memphis" by Marc Cohn. I could name a few others, but these are the songs I've performed the most, and I'm most comfortable with them.

What, if anything, has Karaoke taught you about yourself?
I've learned what a passion I have for music. I knew about it before, but I didn't realize how strong that passion is.

What parallels have you observed between karaoke and other areas of your life?
Every endeavor gets easier the longer you practice and spend time learning and studying the endeavor.

What do people think about karaoke? Do you agree or disagree with their perception?

Most people think it's just something to do when drinking a lot of alcohol—they don't take it very seriously, might even think it's a joke. I think anyone who loves music would see it differently.

How do you incorporate fun into your life? What hobbies do you enjoy?

I like to have as much fun as possible in general both at work and at play. Music, movies, and hanging out with family and friends are the ways I like to spend my time. I also enjoy eating out and attending concerts.

What are the fun aspects of your work life? How do you pursue loving what you do?

Music is huge. Karaoke and concerts are two ways I pursue my love of music. I also play keyboard and piano on occasion as well.

What do you think the karaoke experience offers people? What do you think it gives to you?

Karaoke is a great way to meet new friends who share the same passion for music. It has allowed me to meet some great folks who are fun to spend time with, and it is also a great way to escape the day-to-day grind and relieve stress.

SIN**G**!

Part IV: **G**o For It!

"Playing safe is probably the most unsafe thing in the world. You cannot stand still. You must go forward." —Robert Collier[44]

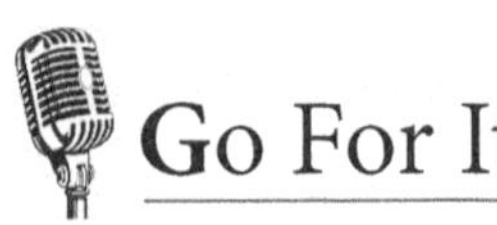
Go For It

Influential speaker and writer Dale Carnegie put it this way: "Inaction breeds doubt and fear. Action breeds confidence and courage. If you want to conquer fear, do not sit home and think about it. Go out and get busy."[45] In other words, don't shrink from the challenge. If you think too much you can begin to shrink back. Thinking equates shrinking but acting leads to impacting. If you want to have a positive impact on the audience don't overthink it.

On karaoke night, if you stop to think, "I wonder if I can hit that note?"—guess what? You probably won't. When we go for it without thinking ourselves backward we will be in a better place mentally and emotionally to face a challenge in the future than if we allowed ourselves to surrender to analysis paralysis. Advance to the next level. Don't hesitate. Go for it. Do not stop short. There's no pause or rewind in life. You either go forward or you expire.

Going for it can also mean physically getting your body moving. The brain, heart, and lungs need blood. The best way to get blood pumping is to move around and get the cardiovascular system going so that you can think more clearly. We hear stories of world leaders who would routinely take a walk during a particular time of day when they had to make a decision. In that process of walking, thinking, talking, and pondering, these powerful people were able to arrive at better decisions than they would if they were just sitting in a room by themselves.

Getting up and moving around is helpful even if you're not a particularly gifted dancer or if you have little sense of rhythm. Many times I've been accused of having zero rhythm and I proudly own that that dubious distinction. Whatever particular goal you have in mind, go for it!

There are legitimate reasons at times to postpone or prepare but never to shrink back. Imagine waking up one morning and signing up for a marathon without having trained adequately beforehand. If the marathon is tomorrow and I say, "I'm not going to do it because I haven't practiced," that doesn't mean I'm not going for it. To go for it in the right way would be to say, "I know there's another race coming up in three months in a town not too far away. I will prepare myself and when that time comes I will be signed up, I will be prepared, and I will go for it." Sometimes it's a matter of timing and preparation, but when the time comes go for it.

 Great Equalizer

I've often equated karaoke with golf. It's my golf, because trust me, I'm not a golfer. If you're not a professional golfer you expect to be fairly poor at the game compared to the pros. And unless you're playing alongside highly skilled amateurs or professionals, the people you hit the course with aren't likely to be amazing golfers either. It's the same dynamic in a karaoke venue. We don't often sing with professional singers or because we ourselves are professional singers. We sing because it's fun.

Participating in karaoke in order to have fun provides a sense of release. It allows me to be present in the moment and enables me to cheer for people I may not have realized had this particular talent or dimension to their personality.

It's an activity that's a great equalizer for people of all estates of life. In an article for the LA Times, a homeless woman from Skid Row summed up the karaoke experience perfectly: "When I perform this song, it opens up my heart and allows me to know that doors may close in my face, but another one opens. And no matter what, I'm not ashamed."[46] The confidence she describes comes from the willingness to be both vulnerable and daring. It

At karaoke night, we're all on a level playing field. People of all ages, incomes, and backgrounds are able to participate equally. It's a remarkable way to bridge an age gap or generation gap. It doesn't matter if you're wealthy or poor, old or young—all that matters is that you have a voice, a willingness to laugh at yourself a little bit, a desire to have fun, and an eagerness to enjoy the camaraderie of others.

takes both attitudes—both vulnerability and boldness—working together in harmony to carry us to a place of confidence and security onstage.

I'm much more likely than I was 15 years ago to take my work very seriously—and yet to take myself less seriously. I laugh at myself much more now. The older I get the easier it gets to laugh at myself. Some days all I have to do is look in the mirror!

 ## Gathering

Depending on your personality there are two primary reasons you may gather with your nexus. For people who strongly identify themselves as introverts, avocations are an opportunity gather resources like enjoyment and knowledge into themselves. For "the more the merrier" extroverts, gathering with others often brings them a boost of social energy that they can carry into other areas of life. Extroverts may gather a big group of people around them while introverts may want to seek more anonymity within a gathering or to spend time on a less social activity.

Your gathering can be physical as well as virtual. I think it's one reason Facebook and other social networking platforms have become so popular. People want to be a part of a community whether it's physical or virtual. These gatherings enrich our lives and help us stay connected to others.

Gatherings are integral to the powerful concept of community. As a child of the television generation I remember shows like *The Andy Griffith Show* set in the tiny community of Mayberry, North Carolina, where the characters' lives intersected in familiar and often humorous ways. I also think of the theme song from the series *Cheers* that remind us how great it feels to be back together with familiar people, particularly (for the characters on the show) at one specific neighborhood pub.

We all want to be a part of a community. It could be at the local coffee shop, church, community center, or any number of other locations. The key element that makes it a community is that it's a place where you know others and you are known by them. We want to be a part of a regular gathering of people with a common purpose to share goals, dreams, ambitions, and desires.

Our role within the community varies from one individual to another. We all have unique reasons for why and how we gather with others. The introvert may draw new ideas, deeper connections, and courage to carry on from the gathering.

Sometimes an introvert just needs the enrichment of her or

his inner life to gain strength. As Mariah Carey's song "Hero" suggests, sometimes what we need lies within us—we need only to connect with and draw upon that inner strength.

The extrovert, on the other hand, may feed off the buzz and excitement of the activity and conversation around them. This is why I love to be a part of a gathering just to go in and blow off steam. People around me get it. Most of them are there for the same reason. Karaoke gives me a self-expression opportunity I wouldn't have otherwise. I suppose I could try to just stand on the street corner and sing but the karaoke stage gives me an opportunity to sing with a purpose and passion because I'm participating in a gathering of fellow enthusiasts.

During the business day we benefit from gathering talented teammates around us who complement and contrast our skills. It's *essential* if we want to expand our success. No one individual is a source of all knowledge, skill, and talent. It often takes a team of talented people to accomplish the goals set before us. We must skillfully and patiently identify people who have talents we may not possess. It also takes courage to look at them and say, "I know you're smarter than I am," or "I know you're more talented than I am," and be willing to bring them into the gathering. Yet the worthwhile result is that the team can perform at a higher level than each of us could on our own.

My friend and fellow karaoke enthusiast Bill frequently mentions this quote from the authors of the book *Mavericks at Work:* "Nobody is as smart as everybody."[47] What they went on to explain was that in the creative process, drawing from a variety of different perspectives often brings about the best collective creativity. While one individual may have what seems like a fabulous idea, discussing it with others can serve to sharpen that idea and make it more marketable, practical and valuable.

 Goofiness

Whimsy, silliness and fun all enrich our lives. Likeminded people who are willing to accept our eccentricities can bring those behaviors out in us. They can allow us to let loose in a way that is purposeful and productive. Whimsy and silliness just for their own sake have little value but when they inspire us to creative thought and action, they have tremendous value.

It looks a little different for everybody. You may enjoy paintball or laser tag. You may be an avid video game player. You may go so far as to dress up in costumes and attend ComicCon or engage in fake fighting tournaments (a.k.a. "larping") with your friends. However extreme your personal goofiness goes, it allows you to engage with new possibilities. It's a door to an alternate reality in which this type of behavior is not only accepted but welcomed. Chances are there are other adults out there who would get excited by the prospect of playing in a kickball league or a round of pick-up dodgeball.

One example of embracing goofiness is a competition called Tough Mudder.[48] Participants pay an admission fee to run an obstacle course through the mud as a personal rite of passage or just to prove they are capable of succeeding. And it's not only an obstacle course—it's also an endurance race that stretches over several miles. The only tangible rewards you get at the end are a few small prizes. Nevertheless, the event has really caught on, particularly with professionals between the ages of 20 and 50 who receive little emotional reward from the work they do in their office environments. They want to go out and overcome this muddy series of obstacles so they can get a certificate of completion, a t-shirt, and a couple of beers. There's record enrollment in this event and they're opening Tough Mudder competitions all over the world. More and more people are testing their mettle by tackling this messy and hilarious challenge.

People do these seemingly silly activities so that they can step out of their everyday reality and experience escapism. It allows them to live vicariously in another world through playing a role they wouldn't otherwise. Don't be afraid to embrace goofiness once in a while. It may turn out to be the powerful catalyst that moves you forward to serious success.

# Google Culture

Karaoke singers perfectly exemplify the motto, "work hard, play hard." The seeming insanity of performing onstage at karaoke night helps preserve your sanity so that you can use what you have left during tomorrow's workday. Not having fun is not an option. If you're going to hang out and make an effort why not have the most fun you possibly can?

As a company Google is known for a culture of fun which they illustrate with a company-wide pajama day.[49] Pixar has fairytale-like cottages for offices. Take a lesson from innovative corporations like Google and Pixar along with experiential retailers like Starbucks coffee, Wegmans' supermarkets, or outdoor supplier REI. Create a work culture that includes huge doses of fun. Send employees on adventurous trips, give people opportunities to try new products and experiences, interrupt the everyday routine with activities that your employees and customers will find enjoyable. Guess what? They'll find *working for you* enjoyable, too.

Google allocates a certain amount of "me time"[50] during the work week so that their employees can pursue their own interests while on the clock. What an innovative policy. Truthfully it's very likely that people would take that "me time" out of their working hours anyway so why not allocate it and give them permission? Employees who are having fun are more productive than those who aren't. Being happy and engaged at the workplace leads to higher overall productivity.[51] And if you're more productive you're going to feel a higher sense of satisfaction in your work. Commit to fun. It's a company culture everyone can appreciate.

# Genesis

Maybe you've gotten this far into the book and are thinking, "I don't really get this karaoke thing." That's perfectly okay. Karaoke isn't for everyone (though one can dream, right?). Maybe you want to take up another hobby. Perhaps it's archery or photography, bird-watching or bowling. Whether it's karaoke night or something else entirely, find an avocation that is meaningful to you.

And while you're at it, go back to the beginning. Become a newbie. Seek out people who are interested in the same thing you are, and start fresh by learning from them. Join a nexus of likeminded people so that you can enjoy all the benefits of gathering together. Most importantly gather with others so that you can know them and be known by them. It makes for a very rich time and rewarding experience. It recharges your batteries for those times that you're forced to go it alone. Gathering with others makes being a beginner less intimidating. Be a beginner around others and then when you're ready, bring beginners alongside you. Once you have gained more experience you can be a part of the creative genesis in their lives, too.

 Graze

The best way to develop a new perspective is to graze freely from all the resources around you. Of all the beneficial sources of knowledge and inspiration the greatest is other people. Always seek out opportunities to engage with people who are different from you.

One of my unexpected insights from performing classic songs on karaoke night has been trying to imagine how the original artists must have felt. I try to empathize across time and space with how they were feeling and why they were performing a particular song in a certain way. I also try to connect with the audience and figure out what styles or genres they would like to hear and how I might be able to share my song in a way that appeals to them.

If I'm a barista serving coffee or a person working on a manufacturing line in a factory, my point of view will be different than that of someone who is managing a hundred-person sales team or that of a CEO held accountable daily for the performance of a multi-billion dollar business. The executive knows that her or his career hangs in the balance of whether or not the company achieves certain goals and that their performance has an impact on countless people's livelihoods. Our position in business yields very different perspectives, all of which are important to the overall company culture.

In business, just like in karaoke, we must learn how to have a sense of empathy and how to spend time with people who view life differently than we do.

Intentionally seeking out the company of others, especially those who are different from us, is helpful to us all. It increases our sensitivity for their diverse characteristics and theirs for ours. It also helps us understand how much we can learn from them. Each of us knows something that the person we're sitting with at lunch or over coffee doesn't know. One of the great joys for me whether I'm working as a teacher or as a student is to find out what some of those unique differences are. I have this learning opportunity whenever I meet someone. All it requires of me is to ask, "How can I learn something new? How can I share this new information with others?" Grazing is a wonderful opportunity to take full advantage of the resources around us.

# Great Expectations

At the fresh age of 28, Alexis Dormandy was head of all of all of Virgin Group's new businesses and working directly under the colorful, billionaire-entrepreneur Sir Richard Branson. Of all the lessons he learned in this position, the biggest was, "Set ridiculously high expectations."[52] Even if we don't have any specific designs to become internationally influential multi-industry moguls, it's a fantastic pattern of thinking to embrace.

When we set high expectations for ourselves, our clients will almost always be satisfied with what we deliver. A surprising number of people seem content doing just enough to get by. The bare minimum will not deliver the type of emotional and financial rewards that you will reap if you make the extra effort over time. Attaining respect as a performer, a friend, or a businessperson is a process which demands a great deal of quality time and dedication from each of us.

We see this play out in the life of the so-called "overnight success." Consider the story of singer-songwriter Jewel. How many weeks and months did she sleep in her car, perform in small venues, and try to get a recording contract? Once she became famous, then hey, she's Jewel. But until then who knew her name? It took time and high personal expectations to attain success and recognition.

One helpful goal-setting tool commonly used in business is the acronym S.M.A.R.T.—Specific, Measurable, Attainable (with stretch!), Relevant, and Time-Based.[53] Goals should ideally have all of those different components. Many times people will look at an attainable goal and assume it's like a lay-up—an easy shot. But quite often, it's not like a lay-up; it's a challenge that requires an incredible amount of effort and stretch to be able to reach and maintain.

The good news is that if you set high expectations and ask people to bring their best to each situation, even difficult goals are attainable. Bring your best thinking, your strongest effort, your highest level of collaboration, and your willingness to think about things differently. Hop out of the lockbox that you're in and look at things from a different perspective. Try to see things from your customer's point of view. We all have certain things we need or hope to accomplish in the world—and so do our customers.

In the experience-staging business we ask ourselves, "If I were my customer, what would I want to see?" It's very helpful when you're on stage, too. I know a fellow who professionally coaches entertainers, helping them cultivate their stage presence. He has explained that if you walk up on stage with a mindset that says, "This isn't just about me giving a good performance. This is about me providing something that will excite, energize and delight myself and the crowd," it shifts your entire focus. When you're not self-conscious you're able to focus instead on inspiring the audience to new heights.

Most of the time the people you're leading or teaching will rise to the occasion. In our best performances we always strive to set, maintain, and even exceed great expectations.

 # Gems

Gems are a helpful metaphor for things of value. These "gems" are usually small and unexpected. People are often surprised to be the recipient of a gemstone and in much the same way, if a product, relationship or performance has high value and comes from an unexpected place, it's a gem. Just like a diamond ring given with a marriage proposal, a well-timed gem can change the lives of both the giver and the recipient forever. In avocational pursuits we find gems hidden in the personalities of people around us and in the memories we make together and treasure for a lifetime. In business we always want to be on the lookout for hidden gems of connection and opportunity that can bring great value to our working relationships and career success.

At karaoke night I've often been pleasantly surprised by "gem" performances when I least expected them. There are gems all around you. Be on the lookout for them. You never know what hidden value you may discover.

 # Gel

It's fun to watch the dynamic in a group over time and observe the gradual change in how the different personalities interact with one another. Eventually the presence of someone new or the absence of someone who is normally there has an impact on the gathering. As time passes and familiarity increases people begin to gel and have more fun playing, talking, and joking around together.

It's also interesting to watch someone who has worked for years to develop a craft and to see their performance coalesce or gel into something spectacular. You see this in live performances when each person in a band hits their mark and enters the song with a different instrument at just the right time. The result is bigger than what any one of those individuals could do alone. The song becomes bigger than the band.

When something gels there's an element of the unexpected. Take the literal meaning of the word "gel." If you were to make gelatin, it's something liquid that turns into something solid. Yet it's not completely solid. It's delicate and can be ruined if you get it near a source of heat or knock it over. It can immediately lose that seemingly solid shape it was in before. The moment that everything comes together is not always as solid as it seems. It's tenuous at best and does not last forever.

I've seen sales organizations come together and gel. These were people who thought they could accomplish any task, objective, or challenge set before them. They solidified together through a number of factors—the power of belief, the willingness to prepare, the tangible skills they possessed, the offering they had to present to their customers. Yet I've also seen circumstances destroy organizations that had once seemed solid but were in fact, more vulnerable than anyone realized. People still look back to these situations and say, "Remember that? We thought we could do anything and we were right. We thought it would last forever but we were wrong."

You can't hold everything together and keep the dynamic from changing in every successful season. It's inevitable that nothing lasts forever. The best course of action is to embrace the here and now, enjoy it, and encourage others with a shared set of values and a sense of humor about yourselves. Part of the sweetness of any given moment is knowing that it won't last forever.

Gelling is like any other ephemeral phenomenon of life. When you start counting the days and realize you have fewer days ahead of you than have already passed, the days become sweeter. You know you have to live them to their fullest because they won't always be here. That's why you look at today and say, "Today gelled very nicely. Today is a good day." We're hopeful that tomorrow will be a good day, too.

Gravitas

Gravitas is a presence, a weightiness, a sense of being that projects outward to others in a way that is memorable and meaningful. It portrays confidence and charisma. A person who has gravitas is not someone who necessarily seeks it out but rather develops it through life experience. This person often possesses a desire to continue to improve to and stretch himself or herself over time. People who acquire gravitas do so by being open to challenges that come their way expectedly or unexpectedly, and they are able to handle difficulties with grace and aplomb.

People with gravitas have their own individual gravity. They're grounded. They have their feet firmly planted and won't be moved by the winds of change. No matter what, they're going to be steady and stay the course. It's a compelling characteristic to observe. It's a worthwhile goal to pursue gravitas as you continue to develop your confidence and sense of self both onstage and in life. When you exude gravitas people will sit up and take notice.

Is there someone in your work life who exudes gravitas? What aspects of their personality or business practices exemplifies this quality?

In what areas do you want to feel more grounded?

Greet

It feeds the emotional side of everyone to feel welcomed and to have someone greet you in a way that is sincere and personalized not just a one-size-fits-all salutation. We're greeted a lot when we walk into retail stores. "Hi, how are you today?"

they will usually ask. Yet seldom does that salesperson stop to hear your response nor do you even assume they expect one. And between strangers passing in public there's usually no kind of greeting exchanged at all.

The "Hi, how are you?" and "Fine, how are you?" greeting is very rote, trivial, and has little impact on how our day goes. Meaningless greetings have little relevance to what's going on in our lives. Contrast that empty exchange with the greeting of someone who is especially dear to you who has been away for a number of years. After you have eagerly anticipated their return to the airport or bus station or knocking at your front door, your excitement and sincere joy overflow at the sound of their greeting.

Greetings can be powerful or forgettable. It's valuable to us whether at work or at play to remember that our greeting has an impact on the person receiving it. The quality of a greeting can mean the difference between causing joy or pain for a person and we may not even realize or remember it. I knew someone who used to say, "How ya doin,' handsome?" That was the standard greeting he gave. How much different this greeting is than a generic, "How's it going?" Another greeting I distinctly remember someone saying is, "I am so happy to see you today." A complimentary greeting can make you feel great. Even if the person greeting you is not 100% sincere, you still feel the positive impact.

If you haven't seen someone in a while, hearing "I missed you!" makes you feel appreciated. I experienced this one recent Friday when I went to sing karaoke. People said, "We haven't seen you in a month! It's great that you're here. We're glad you're back." Be thoughtful in the way you greet others. It's a small detail that makes a big difference.

 # Global

Business and entertainment have become global enterprises. Often we'll have people in our audience with different sensibilities, cultural markers, faiths, and customs. Being sensitive to those differences and recognizing that we're now in a global economy and entertainment age is essential to our success as business people.

Karaoke is a global phenomenon. People from countries around the world gather with others to take the stage and belt out their favorite songs in their respective languages and dialects. It's fun to be part of an avocation popular the world over. Maybe I'm singing the same song that a person in Tokyo, London, Manila, or Hong Kong is performing at the same time! The activities we enjoy connect us with more than our small group of friends—they open us up to a worldwide stage!

 # Green Light

We all look for signals in life and the green light means go. It's always helpful to have a green light when you're slowed down or held back. Many of us find it frustrating when we don't have a clear signal for what to do next. There are several green lights that encourage us to keep going when we're performing on the karaoke stage. These may include the audible praise of your audience or enthusiastic shouts of what song to perform next. In the business setting you may look to other side of the table and see your listeners nodding in agreement or asking you to tell them more. In every area of life you see the signals of open body language or hear positive feedback. These are all green lights that can signal to you to keep proceeding in the same direction.

Can you remember a time when you had a green light to move forward and didn't go? If so, what was the result of stalling your forward motion?

Besides direct verbal encouragement what other types of feedback do you look for to give you a green light to move ahead in life and work?

 # Guide

We all need people in our lives who can find not only a way but can also help us find the *best* way to proceed. Each and every guide plays a key role in our attempt to go forward. A guide is another word for a mentor. When we have these guides around us we can have confidence to try things we might not try on our own.

Sometimes when I'm driving, particularly if it's just past sunset and I've flipped the headlights on in the car, I think, "If I didn't have these headlights, I'd probably crash." Even though I would still have the same level of driving skill I wouldn't see the guides going before me indicating the way.

Without the headlights I would likely hit a tree, or run off the road, or hit another vehicle or a person or an animal. The headlights serve as a crucial guide to me.

In much the same way each of us have people around us

whether in a business or performance setting who serve as guides to help us go freely forward in the direction of our choosing. Each of us knows someone in our life who has more education, life experience, common sense, and ability to focus and listen intently than we do. By intentionally committing to spend time with that person whose traits and attributes we admire, we can become more like him or her. In doing so, every one of us can also become a guide or mentor to others.

> *Invest time with a mentor; volunteer time being a mentor. None of us should have to make the journey alone. We have one another as guides.*

 # Gadfly

I am that gadfly which God has given the state and all day long and in all places am always fastening upon you, arousing and persuading and reproaching you.

—Socrates[54]

I have a friend named Wayne who loves to play pranks on people around him. He's something of a gadfly. He loves to provoke, pester, and prank. One of his favorites occurs when we're out at a Mexican restaurant with friends. Wayne will notice when someone at the table is looking away and place a tortilla chip on their shoulder. Then he'll wait 30 seconds and slyly pose a straight-faced question, "What's your problem?" And of course, the person typically responds, "What do you mean? I don't have a problem." "Well," Wayne replies, "you've got a chip on your shoulder!" He's a gadfly and he's fun to be around because he brings a certain levity to gatherings.

Another example would be the good-natured teasing and nicknaming that takes place on karaoke night. Gadflies keep things shaken up. A little unpredictability can make the time more fun and memorable for everyone.

Galvanize

When something is galvanized it's stronger and more protected than it ever would have been before. It's armored against outside forces and inner corrosion.

Galvanizing is a different phenomenon than gelling. Gelling is like a first stage—a weaker solidification than galvanizing—and oftentimes organizations fail to move beyond this delicate starting point. You can see examples of galvanizing—or extra-strength protection against harm—in the example of the life-long friend or the long-term pursuit of an interest, hobby, or career. That's the galvanizing force at play.

You've invested a great deal of care and concern, and as a result, it's not easily damaged or destroyed.

The galvanizing force strengthens communities of people who share a common purpose. Their guiding principle or vision protects them from forces that would otherwise corrode and wear down a group with a weaker sense of unity. I've seen the galvanizing force strengthen my own karaoke nexus over the years we've spent together. It's different than something that has gelled tenuously together which can dissolve and sort of lose its former shape. In this case it takes a whole lot more to tear the galvanized structure apart.

It's an exciting and wonderful experience when something galvanizes. Our relationships and identities can become so strong that we may remain close with others over a long period of time—maybe even a lifetime. The goal in marriage is a galvanizing of spirit between husband and wife so that no matter what happens, outside forces cannot break you apart. You're tough, you're strong, and you're reinforced. No matter how soft you are on the inside, you're tough on the outside.

When you're going after a personal or professional goal, there's a sense of security in knowing you're part of a galvanized union or organization. You feel as if you can take on anything the world sends your way.

 # Gratitude

Every day is a gift. Every wrinkle, line, and headache is a gift. If I notice the years wearing me out, it means that I am still alive, I'm still pursuing the day, and I'm still chasing after the things that matter to me. It's a state of mind that makes all the difference. When I do (and once in a while, I do) slip into an attitude of ingratitude and think about what I could gain or may have missed out on, it's gratitude that brings me back.

Many times what I *actually* receive in life will be less than what I hope or expect to receive. If my expectations are managed in light of reality versus what *might* be possible in some distant fantasy world, I can maintain a sense of gratitude. Being thankful for the moment and not watching the clock or thinking beyond it to the next day makes a big difference. I do anticipate the future but not from a place of impatience with the present. I allow the sense of anticipation to motivate me to prepare.

There are a limited number of opportunities for meaningful endeavors regardless of our stage of life. We trade our time for relationships and monetary reward. We exchange our time for intellectual pursuits and hobbies. We trade it for gathering together with people of the same faith or value system as well as for a number of different tangible and intangible benefits. Make these exchanges wisely and stay grateful for these opportunities. You can't go back and redo them.

I always want to keep a deep sense of gratitude alive and be quick to show my gratitude to others. Whether it's making an appreciative comment, picking up a check, generously tipping the server, giving a round of applause, or initiating a standing ovation, karaoke night provides many chances for both the performer and the audience to show genuine gratitude.

 Group

Like a neighborhood or community, it's always fun to be a part of a group. "Group" signifies familiarity between people, and in that regard it has value both to society at large and to individuals within the smaller, tight-knit group.

Each of us finds different aspects we enjoy about a particular venue and the group of people who frequent it. The first step in finding your group is to understand what you like and don't like and your most comfortable environment. Over the years I've found several places I like and KJs I enjoy but I've also found places I didn't like so much. We tend to gravitate toward places where people want to know us and we want to know more about them, too. Find your place and plug in. Once you do, you can contribute to the group and look forward to coming back week after week.

We enjoy the show when we're a part of a group because when we're all together we create something more than what each of us could do on our own. The same principle applies during the workday. When you assemble a team of individuals who have strengths and talents that complement yours you all begin to work in harmony. As a group you can all create something that is more powerful and relevant to your customers than you would be able to deliver on your own.

Taking the stage in front of a group quickly becomes a significant focal point for your week. It's a great way to unplug and recharge at the end of an exhausting season or a stress-filled day. It can lead to enormous amounts of fun and to lifelong friendships. I've seen this happen to others and have grown much closer to several friends because we have this hobby in common. It's surprising but we can relate other life events to experiences to memories we've made at a certain venue with a group of people. Listening to others in the group or performing a particular song for them becomes a shared experience. People who don't go to karaoke night (even just to cheer from the audience) may never experience what it feels like to have such a group to call their own.

 # Generosity

Generosity is a gift. It affords us the satisfaction of bringing pleasure and joy to others. Be generous as you chase after your pursuits whether they be business-related, avocational, or personal. In doing so, those pursuits will have much more meaning to you and other people will seek you out as a friend, mentor, and go-to performer. Be generous with time as a listener, and also be generous with encouragement and praise. Even being generous with material goods and treasures can make you feel wealthy.

It's the message we all hear around the holidays: It is more blessed to give than to receive. Along with that there's a popular axiom in business: Don't ask, but give. By giving, and giving again, a person opens himself up to getting something in return. Giving has attracted a great deal of buzz in the last few years. If you visit business blogs, particularly sites by entrepreneurial or motivational speakers like Tony Robbins or Ken Blanchard, they will typically have a free offer available. It might be free online-only content, an offer for a newsletter, or a premium item that they ship to you. What they ask from you in return is your contact information. This exchange is not based on traditional purchasing but on giving and giving back. It's the notion of a back-scratching economy. I'll scratch yours, you scratch mine.

It's not about the sell anymore. Selling is practically passé. It's about giving and getting in return. Each of us has something to give.

It's important to prepare your gift properly. You may think of a little girl who makes something with her hands for her parent as a gift. While the gift is heartfelt and endearing, we wouldn't expect whatever she makes to be of the same quality and appearance as something made by a master craftsman. At the same time, we would recognize that she's giving the best she has to offer with the skills and knowledge she possesses. Flash forward twenty years and if that same person gives a spray-painted cigar box "jewelry case" with stuck-on macaroni noodles as a Christmas present, we might not be quite as appreciative of that gift. Cultivate excellence in your craft. Once you achieve excellence, give from that excellence.

Getting is not a successful strategy. Giving, whether in a marriage or a parent-child relationship, is far more rewarding. Always seeking what you can get from someone else is a very selfish approach. The amazing thing about giving is that it actually results in gains over time. If everyone's giving, everybody wins. Getting for its own sake is a lousy motivation. It inevitably breaks down because it is always subtractive. If we're committed to continually giving, we will reap the rewards of continually getting at the same time.

On karaoke night the best performers are those who give freely to the audience. A well-rehearsed performance gives many benefits to the performer as well, including a sense of competency, accomplishment, and exhilaration. In the giving we get—which is a paradox we can all enjoy.

 # Grow

Stretching yourself contributes to growth as does taking on new challenges. Settling into a rut hampers growth. If you're not taking time to learn new things and stretch yourself in new ways, life becomes gray and boring. When we indulge this kind of thinking we are essentially saying that we've arrived and don't need to grow anymore. It's a depressing notion since the next logical step would be to say that we're going to just breathe until we die because we've done all we can do. That type of existence is dark and empty. How much better it is to commit to lifelong learning and personal growth. Without the sense of purpose that comes from daring ourselves to be the best we can be, to give to others, and to try new things, we miss out on many enriching opportunities.

Growth is not an instant phenomenon. It's a process. Don't expect to be great your first time on stage. If by some fluke you're able to pull greatness out of thin air on your first attempt, don't expect to maintain it. Energy and bravado can carry you to a certain level but it's through hours of practice and the commitment to improve that eventually you can deliver greatness on a consistent basis. There's a time-honored principle of learning that when you first encounter new material you're at the level known as "unconscious incompetence."[55] What this means is that there are things you don't know *that you don't even realize* you don't know. In other words, you're ignorant of your ignorance.

As you begin to learn you become "consciously incompetent." You are now aware of your ignorance in a particular area. The next stage is "conscious competence." You've become familiar with a specific body of work, you've learned some material, or you've mastered some skill. But in order to show what you know, you consciously refer back to what you've learned. It's a state of knowing what you know and how to share it.

The final level of learning, or mastery, is when you become "unconsciously competent." What you've learned is now part of you. Your knowledge becomes integrated fully into who you are from that point forward. You see this clearly with virtuoso musicians whose guitar or piano seems like an extension of their body.

Several years ago we observed this at an NBA game while watching Michael Jordan play. They say, "be the ball"—and it honestly seemed like the ball was part of him. He had unrivaled control and mastery over it. We've seen it in concerts where artists are seemingly unconscious or "in the zone" on the stage, and as a result, they're performing at a high level that excites and delights the audience.

Sadly, many people seem to live without the drive to keep growing day in and day out simply because they don't know any better. Perhaps they had a lackluster example handed down to them by their parents and grandparents. If this is you I encourage you to tell yourself, "No matter where I'm starting from, I can grow. There are things I can learn, changes I can make, and ways I can challenge myself."

When we stop seeking out opportunities to grow we're essentially resigning to a slow death. If we're not growing we're drying up like a shriveled plant. The moment you say, "I'm not going to learn anything new, or meet anyone new, or try any new challenges, or learn any new skills," a part of you has died.

Neuroscience research confirms[56] that our brains continue to develop throughout the entire span of our lives. As our cognitive abilities expand and increase so should our interests, social connections, hobbies and other pursuits until the very end of life. The good news? It's never too late to outgrow ourselves.

# Generations

Karaoke is a pursuit for multiple generations to participate in and enjoy. It's always fun watching my mom, aunts, and other relatives gather together at family reunions to sing their favorite songs as a group. It usually results in lots of laughter and enthusiastic cheering from the peanut gallery.

As Americans we're particularly challenged when it comes to recognizing the wisdom of older generations. Many of us would prefer to go online to learn about the past rather than have a conversation with someone who has lived through the era we're curious to research. People from older generations have a helpful perspective on the world. They've overcome many of the challenges we face today as younger people.

We also tend to segregate ourselves into groups with people close to our age who are in similar life situations. Narrowing your interactions this way is limiting to both older and younger people alike. An older person can stay young at heart and in mind by conversing with young people and seeing the world through their eyes.

There's value in being able to tap into the wisdom of people of different ages. It helps us understand how they see the world. We can then internalize their point of view for our own benefit. I've come to realize that my perspective is not authoritative. The views and beliefs of other people, particularly from different generations, have validity and worth and they have a positive impact on my own perspective. If we listen carefully and respect what others have to say we can learn a tremendous amount from every generation.

Karaoke's format and culture hearken back to generations before us to how they enjoyed music together. Despite the technology involved, karaoke is arguably our modern equivalent of gathering around a piano and singing together. It brings to mind the great sing-alongs that happen spontaneously when you're with a group of enthusiastic music lovers—maybe when you're sitting around a campfire or on a long road trip.

There are certain instantly recognizable standards whether from classic rock, country, jazz, or hip hop that you hear almost every time you perform karaoke. It's strangely comforting to hear these songs. They generate familiarity and connection to the past. There's a sense of belonging that you feel when you're with people who don't just tolerate hearing these same songs but actually anticipate   them as the "golden oldies" of karaoke. People smile when they hear "Piano Man" by Billy Joel, 'Total Eclipse of the Heart" by Bonnie Tyler, or "Don't Stop Believin'" by Journey. Each of these songs is like a treasured piece of art to many people yet with the comfort and familiarity of a favorite pair of blue jeans.

Deeply embedded in these songs is a sense that we're here and this is what we do, and this is how it feels. The karaoke standards remind me how glad I am to be here each time I hear or sing them. I'm grateful for another performance of these same songs by these familiar people who respect these tried-and-true artists. I know I may not be here again but I'm here right now. Karaoke night becomes a very powerful escapist and metaphysical sensation. We can reach across time and space and unite with people who have been there before and might be there in the future.

 # Good

What makes something good? At the risk of sounding overly philosophical, it's a very important question to consider if we want to go forward.

Good times can be times that are fun, times that are good *for* us, or ideally both. It is entirely possible to have fun and to contribute to others in a positive way at the same time. Good times keep us from becoming overly consumed with only work or serious subjects. Participating in a gathering of people who enjoy one another and share an affinity for the activity at hand are vital ingredients for a good time. We want to keep that whimsical side alive and keep ourselves open to opportunities for fun in life. As I've said before, you never want to kill the kid inside of you. Keep him alive and help him thrive!

I recently attended a conference in Orlando centered around creativity, innovation, and imagination. One of the presenters commented that after the age range of 5 to 7 years old, most people begin to be very serious and lose some of the playfulness they had as little children. In order to counter that overly serious "adult" mode of thinking, each member of our groups attempted an unusual exercise. We were each asked to explain the work we do so that a 5-year-old could understand it. The result was fascinating because it forced us to do away with business-speak and pretense. We had to set aside our usual professionalism to very simply explain to those around us what it is we do to earn money. It was a very enlightening diversion from the same old seriousness and very fun as well.

Breaking away from the expected routine and what's expected once in a while can open us up to more playfulness. On the one hand there's a sense of security in offering the same thing over and over again. We maintain a sense of comfort and competency in delivering the predictable. On the other hand if we provide fresh and creative alternatives alongside these, our customer will view us as being innovative and highly relevant. Continuing to offer the same thing over and over again without alternatives puts us at risk of becoming obsolete and irrelevant to them and their customers. There's no better way to continue to stay fresh and relevant than by stretching ourselves and continually reviewing and improving our performance.

How do you define good quality? Today virtually every company has the capability to develop good products and services. It's a matter of choice. Do they want to produce the best or make something lesser?

They may lower standards to appeal to a market that doesn't demand the highest quality and would rather have a lower price. In this case price is what determines the standard for quality over and above craftsmanship or other quality indicators. Define your standard of excellence and be true to it. Align your goals to your standards for greatness.

> *"My model for business is The Beatles. They were four guys who kept each other's kind of negative tendencies in check. They balanced each other and the total was greater than the sum of the parts. That's how I see business: great things in business are never done by one person, they're done by a team of people."*
> *—Steve Jobs in an interview with 60 Minutes*[57]

If we look at the components of a good show we'll see that it requires great preparation and a strong commitment to both your audience and your craft. A good show is the ultimate goal of an onstage performance as well as a business performance.

Ultimately, the good stuff isn't really about stuff. Over time, one of the key differentiators between what is or isn't good is your team of people. Enthusiastic, talented people working toward a set of goals who narrow their focus to a specific offering and specific customer market make all the difference. Technology, production capabilities, or raw material capability don't make the difference—people do.

Interpersonal skills and emotional intelligence matter. It's a true talent to recognize how others can complement your strengths and shore up your weaknesses. Great teachers instructing by candlelight and using an abacus will yield better results than teachers working in a lavish, high-tech environment if they have no passion, dedication, or personal insight. It is impossible to deliver a good product or performance without the contributions of good people. People make the difference.

 # Games

Games are a fun way to explore our potential as competitors. They are an avenue to test out different behaviors within the guardrails of the game's structure and rules. In gaming situations you have far fewer consequences than you do in real life. Games allow us to take on different identities, assume alternate lives, or tackle new challenges that we might not normally attempt. They open us up to opportunities for risk without severe repercussions.

Games are good for us. There's a highly entertaining game called Kamikaze Karaoke, and it works like this. Rather than putting in a song you know you feel comfortable singing, the KJ selects a song at random for you. It may or may not be in your range or repertoire or be something you are sure you can perform well.

Nevertheless, if you're playing the game you've got to step

up and sing. It's an often hilarious exercise that takes you out of your comfort zone (it certainly does for me) but doesn't have any lasting negative consequences.

Kamikaze Karaoke, like most games, is just a fun and unusual opportunity to learn a new song and break out of the ordinary for a while.

During baseball playoffs, one mistake on the part of the pitcher can result in a change of the game in favor of the other team. Likewise, one brilliant insight on the part of the hitter can result in a change of the game in favor of his team. While performing in business or entertainment every decision we make can change the game even if only in subtle ways. The cumulative effect of these tiny decisions at the end of the day may result in a dramatically different outcome. We're largely unaware of the effect of the decisions we make.

The movie *"Groundhog Day"* clearly illustrates this idea. The main character, Phil Connors (played by Bill Murray), has the unwelcome opportunity to relive the same day over and over again for a period that the movie's director estimated to be about 30-40 years.[58] For a while, Phil keeps living the deja-vu day in basically the same way. But after he has repeated the day several hundred times he begins to make changes—small tweaks at first and then eventually bigger ones. The changes he makes ultimately yield a completely different outcome at the end of that very long, repeated day.

We have a similar opportunity in our lives to change important outcomes through the choices we make on a daily basis. Moment by moment each decision can be a game-changer. Do we choose to speak a word of encouragement or a hasty one in anger? What is the result of that word not only in that moment but over the long-term relationship? How does it change us as people if we give into a negative impulse rather than exercising patience? Even a small difference in our intentions and actions can significantly change the game.

# Groove

The word "groovy," a 1960s term for something desirable or cool, comes from the grooves on the surface of a record.[59] When the needle touches the groove and the record rotates the friction creates music in the groove. Groovy describes any activity or gathering that has an element of attraction or excitement to it. It's also an integral part of my stage persona— the Groove Doctor.

Being in the groove is similar to the concept of "flow."[60] When you're in the groove, things that were once difficult become easy. Things that were fast suddenly slow down. You move forward effortlessly, you're hitting all the right notes, you're perceiving all the right insights. When you're in the groove, you understand the audience very well, you have a sense of ease and relaxation, and you immerse yourself fully in enjoying the moment.

Karaoke has a long list of positive attributes. It's fun, it's readily available, and it's inexpensive. It can be a team or individual activity, it fosters a supportive environment, and it tests each performer's ability to engage the audience. To me these aspects are what make it fun. There's a certain purity to karaoke. It's a form of participatory entertainment, and very few performers have the expectation that they'll take it to some next level. There's no monetary or competitive incentive to say, "I've got to be good and you've got to be bad." On karaoke night people cheer each other on toward success. We're all in this together and we're all here to have a good time getting our groove on.

There are plenty of songs that get you in the mood to party. That's a great mindset to have—to tell yourself, "I'm here for the party." I'm here to have a great time, blow off some steam, to meet new people, hear some great singers, and enjoy our time together. When I go into work tomorrow I'll be a more relaxed, energetic, and creative person as a result of showing up for karaoke night tonight.

New Orleans is a karaoke lover's dream town, especially singing at Cat's Meow on Bourbon Street. If you're familiar with New Orleans, there's a good chance it's because of their Mardi Gras celebrations. Mardi Gras is a French phrase that translates to "Fat Tuesday." It's essentially an enormous party they throw the day before Ash Wednesday when many Christians start the 40-day fast for Lent. One famous Mardi Gras tradition is the King Cake—a delicious dessert that contains a little plastic baby that represents the Baby Jesus. He's swimming in the batter somewhere. The King Cake tradition offers us a perfect illustration of celebrating life to the fullest. Becoming immersed in the moment, letting go, not holding back, and fully involving yourself in the activity and the energy of the people around you leads to that sense of celebration. The baby in

The groove captures a particular snapshot of life—the moment in time when everything falls into place. There's no pressing awareness of how old, rich, smart, or whatever else you are. You're just there as yourself in the moment, you're in the flow, and it's wonderful.

the King Cake has the right idea. He's fully immersed, fully in the moment, and ready for the celebration.

Time and space seem to come together in just a matter of a few minutes in which you feel totally at peace. The groove is a place we continually want to return to and enjoy. It calls out from the both the chaos and the tedium of life until we find it again.

 # Gains

Where would you like to make gains in life? Every day presents new and varied opportunities. Studying in a classroom results in intellectual gains. Working out in a gym results in physical gains. Participating in activities that make us uncomfortable at first eventually result in confidence gains.

If we're not continuing toward self-improvement, we'll not only miss out on gains that propel us ahead, we'll actually begin to recede. The opposite of a gain isn't standing still or remaining neutral, it is backsliding or losing progress. We must continue to seek out opportunities to grow, expand, and gain in every area of our lives.

A few years ago a fellow karaoke enthusiast showed up one karoke night with only two or three songs he felt comfortable singing. After a few months he was up to just over a dozen songs in his repertoire. Now about five years later he has close to 600 songs he can sing confidently and comfortably. He's made some real gains in that area. Other people can help you see the gains you're making and how to go further than you thought you could before. Ask some questions, find out where you're making progress, and keep it up!

 # Guests

There's something about the word "guest" that conveys a sense of welcome rather than imposition. When someone describes another person as the " customer" or "patron" instead of as the guest it seems as if that individual is somehow permanently attached to a transaction.

I like to think about it this way. You'd never invite a guest show up at your doorstep only say to them, "Okay, pay me a dollar," or "What did you bring me?" or "Why are you here?" Yet oftentimes that's how we treat customers and clients. "What can I get from you?" we ask with our attitude and word choice. It's the opposite of that generous giving mentality. Instead of being hospitable and others-focused, we fixate on what can get from others.

If someone is our guest our goal is to serve them. Just as with giving to others, in serving our guests we receive from them in return. Perhaps Lumiere the candlestick and his ensemble of anthropomorphic dishes said it best in Disney's *"Beauty and the Beast"* when he sang the song, "Be Our Guest."[61] Everyone in your audience is your guest and should be respected and honored as though you personally invited them to be there. Your performance invites them and encourages them to make themselves at home and enjoy the show.

If you treat your audience as your guests you have the pleasure of acting as the host. A host is hospitable and invites the guests to partake in the good time. It's a shared experience rather than a transaction. Transactions are a dime a dozen. When I am performing, I want the audience to have fun with me. I don't mind if they laugh at me if they're enjoying the good time. And of course, I certainly don't mind if they stand up and cheer!

 # Grassroots

Grassroots performances, audiences, and publicity are all part of what happens when people gather as a neighborhood, community, or nexus. The participants have fun and want to tell others about it and get them involved in the process. If it remains an authentic not-for-profit pursuit it will grow and eventually become a grassroots movement. There's often unexpected power inherent to grassroots movements. If you've got a gathering of people with shared authentic enthusiasm, it's a force that can have an incredible impact on the world.

Enough movement within a grassroots gathering can cause a ground swell. A ground swell is similar to the tipping point[62] described by best-selling author Malcolm Gladwell. A ground swell is when a movement, belief, or form of entertainment reaches a critical mass. At that point people begin to participate in large numbers. It's when the masses begin to understand the reason why this thing is attracting so many enthusiasts. A ground swell doesn't have to be limited to business or entertainment exclusively. It could happen anywhere there's an organic, passionate movement toward something.

In our business we're seeing a ground swell within the area of specialty food. Rapidly increasing numbers of people are participating in dining clubs, specialty festivals, and pop-up dinners. Gourmet food halls like Eataly in New York City,

Chicago, and other cities, attract foodies by the thousands. Numerous examples abound in other areas of interest such as community singing groups and choirs, or small fellowship groups based out of large churches. The primary momentum behind this kind of movement is positive word of mouth, a desire for community, and the endorsement from friends and experts who say, "This is really something you ought to try." The end result is that all these tiny gatherings create huge movements in their own spheres of influence. The connections we make with people during our free time—at karaoke night, book club on the golf course, or around a campfire—can expand outward to change the world on a much bigger scale. Just like the legend claims that the flutter of butterfly wings in one area of the world causes a tsunami in another,[63] many people uniting in small ways can metaphorically cause a grassroots movement to become a ground swell.

 Get Over Yourself

Geting over yourself begins with generally taking yourself less seriously. I've listened to people who sing with great affectation and styling who seem to be very impressed with their own vocal abilities and I find it alternately amusing and sad. The ability to enjoy the music for the sake of the music is the main thing, not desperately trying to show everyone how awesome you think you are.

Next in line after the love of music should be the effort to serve the audience and deliver something they will enjoy. When I'm on stage it's not about me. It's not about my ego or having to prove something to myself or my friends. I do appreciate all the benefits I derive from the experience but it's really not about me. If you need to boost your ego or take up all the attention in the room there may be something out of balance in your life. You can't use the stage to correct past injustices or sing your way out of long-past disappointments. Make it about the audience. Make it about enjoying the moment. For a positive experience to happen you've got to get over yourself.

Karaoke is a perfect activity to practice getting over yourself. It is most welcoming to participants who are willing to let loose. As one karaoke enthusiast put it, "I love karaoke not for the singing but for the performance…It gives me an excuse to scream at the top of my lungs." He's got the right idea—entertainment over ego.

The reality is performances are never perfect. No two performances are ever the same. In light of this truth we always want to remember the commonsense mantra about balancing our priorities: Take your work seriously, but don't take yourself so seriously.

Be willing to laugh at yourself and be willing to laugh *with* but never *at* others. There's a key distinction here. Most of us can remember a time in life when we've been laughed at, perhaps sometime in childhood, and how painful that experience can be. It's easy to laugh at the mistakes of others but it's not always easy to laugh at ourselves. We're all naturally wired to defend ourselves and criticize others. Resist this impulse.

If others are laughing at themselves and invite us to laugh along with them that's fine. But I'm adamantly opposed to laughing at others. I admire individuals for being brave enough to step up on stage, whether a musical stage or business stage, and to show the world what they can do. I admire that simple willingness to "just do it"[64] as Nike would say, and I refuse to laugh at them even if they don't possess the level of skill or competency that I would like to see. If they're willing to step up, to make the move in a positive direction, it's likely that after some time and practice, they will be unstoppable. They will develop the skills, polish, and confidence that they need to put on a really good show. They will learn what it takes to deliver a high level of service or stage a fantastically engaging guest experience.

Don't take yourself too seriously. Take your work very seriously. Don't take the perfect performance seriously—you'll miss out on enjoying the experience. Go out there and have fun. If you've prepared, you'll be able to entertain and engage both yourself and your audience. Get over yourself and go for it!

 # Glue: The Stickiness Factor

Recently, I went about a month without singing karaoke. It was awful! I knew I needed that creative outlet—and frankly, I knew I needed that chance to cut loose and shout out requests and sing my favorite songs at the top of my lungs. As soon as I walked into the venue that night I was immediately greeted by smiles, warm handshakes and hugs. *Doc is back.* "It's so good to see you!" they said. "Where have you been? What have you been doing?" It felt good to know I had been missed.

There's a profound stickiness to a gathering like that. You can sense some relational glue between people who notice when you're there and miss you when you're absent. That glue is a substantial component to any gathering. The positive emotions your gathering generates for everybody involved form the stickiness and glue that hold your nexus together and lend it staying power.

Which coworkers or friends act as the glue that keeps your nexus together? What characteristics do these "glue" people possess that we appreciate and feel ourselves drawn to?

How might the stickiness factor impact your ability to go for your personal performance objectives or life goals?

 # Glow

Winston Churchill once said, "We are all worms, but I do believe that I am a glow worm."[65] I always took that to mean that if you do things that are extraordinary and that excite others, people will begin to notice a certain glow or charisma about you that is desirable and that they want to be around.

Emanate warmth and personal charity. People will be drawn to that glow and will want to gather around it as they would around a blazing hearth on a cold winter's day. When you glow in the midst of others, your presence becomes a catalyst for community and a conduit for good.

One of the very best compliments I've ever received in a business setting happened a few years ago when someone said to me, "We just like to be around you because you make other people feel good." That's an incredible privilege—to make other people feel good about being them. Go forward and glow brightly.

 Gear Up

When you select the right gear on a bicycle or a truck, you can maximize your effort and more easily gain momentum. But when it comes to our vocation or avocation, what do we really mean by "momentum"?

There are times in life when you have to gear up for action. Many sports commentators use the word momentum to describe the increasing intensity of an athletic event. When one of the teams appears to be doing things right and getting all the breaks we see their momentum build. Yet it's probably not sheer luck that's propelling the triumphant team forward but rather a combination of strategy and determined effort.

Momentum is achieved through constancy of effort and purpose. Momentum isn't magical. It's the culmination of preparation and dedication over an extended period of time. It's exciting and rewarding to see momentum kick in. It's when we see high-level competency in action. Anytime someone's performance at work or onstage seems excellent but utterly unconscious we witness momentum in action. We see a person who is able to do what they set out to do succeed without having to think step-by-step about what they're trying to accomplish. It takes preparation and commitment to gear up to that extraordinary type of momentum.

 Gold Standard

There was a time when all of our monetary system was backed with gold. At any time you wished you could redeem paper currency or coins for their equal value in gold. Today we have a fiat currency, that is, one that's based exclusively on our trust in our nation's economy and the values they assign to money and we could not redeem our Federal Reserve notes or coins for an equal amount of gold. Nevertheless, we still use that expression, the gold standard.

In the same way, I can redeem the gifts and assets that I have for value from other people. To me that's the ultimate gold standard. Resources of the highest value are found within human beings. I give a valuable gift to my guests or audience and in return I eagerly expect to receive from them the gifts that they have to offer.

"Gold standard" also refers to a measure of the highest quality. In the music industry artists know they've truly "arrived" when they finally earn a gold record for their record sales. We often view the greatest possible level of achievement as the gold standard and compare other values against its example. It's a helpful benchmark to keep in mind in the midst of any pursuit. Whether in our personal lives, business dealings, or passionate pursuits on a stage of any kind, it's wise for us to pause and think, "How can I take myself to that gold-standard level?" If you and I continue to seek excellence, we're ensuring that those around us are investing their one irretrievable resource—their time—in a valuable way.

Keep seeking. Keep up the hard yet good work of pursuing excellence in your living, giving, and performing. Don't settle for anything less on the stage of life—go for the gold!

Your **Go** for It Track List:

1. Walk This Way—Aerosmith
2. The Distance—Cake
3. Kind and Generous—Natalie Merchant
4. Celebration—Cool and the Gang
5. Party Hard—Andrew W.K.
6. Here For the Party—Gretchen Wilson
7. Tell Me Something Good—Rufus and Chaka Khan
8. Halo—Beyonce
9. Heart of Gold—Neil Young
10. Give a Little Bit—Supertramp

What other Go for It tracks are on your list?

____

____

____

____

Rehearsal Notes

1. What are three goals I want to "go for" in the next 90 days?

____

____

____

____

2. Have you ever experienced a group gelling during a fun or goofy activity? Describe the experience here.

____

____

____

____

3. List some ideas or activities that might galvanize your organization or group. Think creatively.

____

____

____

____

SING!

Step Up
What could you do if you weren't afraid?
Take the risk. Start today.

Inspire and be Inspired
What energizes and motivates you?
How can you motivate others?

Find Your Nexus
Surround yourself with people with shared
interests, talents, and strengths.

Go for It!
What is your stage? Put the lessons to work on
your life stage.

**Keep up with Doc and the latest Karaoke
happenings at www.karaokelifelessons.com**

FOOTNOTES

[1] http://www.funnyordie.com/videos/4a87d48fdd/undercover-karaoke-withjewel

[2] http://www.forbes.com/sites/susanadams/2012/05/18/new-survey-majority-of-employees-dissatisfied/

[3] http://www.redbookmag.com/fun-contests/celebrity/beyonce-knowles-interview

[4] http://www.ted.com/talks/david_kelley_how_to_build_your_creative_confidence.html

[5] http://www.forbes.com/sites/mikemyatt/2013/02/08/the-power-of-what-if/

[6] http://news.bbc.co.uk/onthisday/hi/dates/stories/may/6/newsid_2511000/2511575.stm

[7] http://money.ca.msn.com/small-business/gallery/18-tips-for-success-from-richard-branson-1?page=4

[8] http://www.chicagotribune.com/classified/jobs/chi-face-your-fear-of-public-speaking-20130614,0,3573369.story

[9] http://www.ted.com/talks/tim_brown_on_creativity_and_play.html

[10] http://www.rollingstone.com/music/lists/100-greatest-singers-of-all-time-19691231/james-taylor-20101202

[11] www.jamestaylor.com/biography

[12] http://www.esquire.com/features/what-ive-learned/woody-allen-0913

[13] http://www.innovationexcellence.com/blog/2011/08/16/25-inspiring-innovation-quotes/

[14] http://www.storytelling-in-business.com/about/

[15] http://www.seriousplay.com/

[16] http://www.imdb.com/title/tt0109686/quotes

[17] http://www.huffingtonpost.com/susan-ann-darley/creativity-_b_3729209.html

[18] http://kids.niehs.nih.gov/games/songs/movies/whistlemp3.htm

[19] http://www.oprah.com/quote/Ralph-Waldo-Emerson-Quote-What-Lies-Behind-Us

[20] http://www.forbes.com/sites/carminegallo/2013/08/27/public-speaking-how-mlk-improvised-second-half-of-dream-speech/

[21] http://women2.com/tina-feys-rules-for-improv-and-your-career/

[22] http://www.rollingstone.com/music/lists/the-500-greatest-songs-of-all-time-20110407/aretha-franklin-respect-20110516

[23] http://www.huffingtonpost.com/susan-ann-darley/creativity-_b_3729209.html

[24] http://history1900s.about.com/od/people/a/Frank-Sinatra.htm

[25] http://www.songlyrics.com/frank-sinatra/i-did-it-my-way-lyrics/

[26] http://www.saturdayeveningpost.com/2010/03/20/archives/post-perspective/imagination-important-knowledge.html

[27] http://www.the-secret-of-mindpower-and-nlp.com/Imagining-perfect-performance.html

[28] http://www.iamsecond.com/

[29] http://www.strategichorizons.com/documents/MarketingManagement0108KeepItReal.pdf

[30] http://www.brainyquote.com/quotes/quotes/j/johnfkenn110220.html

[31] http://www.twainquotes.com/Procrastination.html

[32] http://www.winstonchurchill.org/learn/speeches/speeches-of-winston-churchill/103-never-give-in

[33] http://en.thinkexist.com/quotation/if_i_had_eight_hours_to_chop_down_a_tree-i-d/194268.html

[34] http://www.nightingale.com/products/think-grow-rich-napoleon-hill/

[35] http://thinkexist.com/quotation/if-my-mind-can-conceive-it-and-my-heart-can/362008.html

[36] http://gladwell.com/blink/

[37] https://www.grant-thornton.co.uk/en/Thinking/tom_peters_in_search_of_great_leadership/

[38] http://www.phrases.org.uk/meanings/genius-is-one-percent-perspiration-ninety-nine-percent-perspiration.html

[39] http://www.quotationspage.com/quote/35879.html

[40] http://www.pbs.org/wgbh/americanexperience/features/timeline/grant-timeline/

[41] http://entertainment.time.com/2012/06/06/r-i-p-ray-bradbury-he-jumped-off-cliffs-and-never-hit-the-ground/

[42] http://www.entheos.com/quotes/by_topic/Ralph+waldo+emerson

[43] http://www.armedforces.com/enthusiasm-defines-a-true-leader/

[44] http://www.youmotivation.com/inspirational-quotes/30-inspirational-quotes- robert-collier-9104

[45] http://blog.dalecarnegie.com/tipsforsuccess/20-tips-on-overcoming-fear/

[46] http://articles.latimes.com/2012/oct/14/entertainment/la-ca-karaoke-skid-row-20121015/2

[47] http://www.untag-smd.ac.id/files/Perpustakaan_Digital_1/BUSINESS%20Mavericks%20at%20work.p df

[48] http://toughmudder.com/?gclid=CKzhsOW3krwCFWIV7Aoddw8AgQ

[49] http://money.cnn.com/2007/01/05/magazines/fortune/Search_and_enjoy.fortune/

[50] http://www.businessinsider.com/google-employee-favorite-perks-2013-3?op=1

[51] http://pps.sagepub.com/content/5/4/378.abstract

[52] http://www.businessinsider.com/lessons-from-richard-branson-2012-12

[53] http://topachievement.com/smart.html

[54] http://classics.mit.edu/Plato/apology.html

[55] http://www.integratedwork.com/wp- content/uploads/2012/03/7ConsciousCompetenceLearning_022712.pdf

[56] http://margiewarrell.com/neuroplasticity-to-outsmart-your-brain/

[57] http://www.cbsnews.com/videos/steve-jobs-50069236/

[58] http://uk.movies.yahoo.com/blogs/movie-editors/long-bill-murray-stuck-groundhog-day-145726453.html

[59] http://mentalfloss.com/article/29777/jive-talkin'-origins-cool-dudes-groovy-chicks-and-hip-cats

[60] http://psychology.about.com/od/PositivePsychology/a/flow.htm

[61] http://www.disneyclips.com/lyrics/lyrics7.html

[62] http://www.amazon.com/The-Tipping-Point-Little-Difference/dp/0316346624

[63] http://www.livescience.com/17455-butterfly-effect-weather-prediction.html

[64]http://nikeinc.com/news/nike-evolves-just-do-it-with-new-campaign

[65]http://www.nationalchurchillmuseum.org/winston-churchill-leadership-the-glow-worm.html

[i]http://www.quotationspage.com/quote/39942.html

[ii]http://www.news.com.au/finance/highachievers-suffering-from-imposter-syndrome/story-e6frfm1i-1226779707766

[iii]http://www.the-secret-of-mindpower-and-nlp.com/Imagining-perfect-performance.html

[iv]Seth Godin, Tribes (New York: Penguin, 2008), 2.

[v]http://www.inc.com/magazine/201310/leigh-buchanan/why-creativity-is-like-karaoke.html

[vi]http://www.pbs.org/thisemotionallife/topic/connecting/connection-happiness

INDEX

Acknowledgements

This book is, in a very tangible way, a collaborative effort. It is the result of my interactions with thousands of people across hundreds of venues during the past couple of decades. It is also a product of each person who has seen fit to befriend and/or invest in me. It is the result of my family's love and support—and the extraordinary blessings God has bestowed on my life. Though I am sure I'll forget someone, I'd like to thank the following people:

My wife, best friend, business partner, and confidante, Nancy Dragoo for her continued help and support on this project. You make me so much better than I would be without you in my life.

My children, Jason (and our daughter-in-law Rachael), Josh, Stephanie (and our son-in-law Josh). Though they were initial skeptics of my passion for singing in front of strangers in public, they have each become Karaoke practitioners and enthusiasts in their own right.

My Mom & Dad, and my siblings, whose love for life and each other made our home a place filled with love, music and performance.

My in-laws, who laugh at my stupid jokes and ask me to sing Wild Cherry songs.

Mike Hyatt, whose direct encouragement and inspiring example played a significant part in helping me move this book from an idea to a reality.

My Karaoke nexus members, including, but not limited to: Wayne, Mark, Kate, Chris, Bill, Sue, Jillene, Mike, Janette, Crystal, Dwayne, Betsy, Ashley, Stazi, Gordy, Kathleen, Mr. T, Melissa, Vanessa, Larry, Voni, Franco, Patti, Char, Jack, Dave, Jerry, Al, Brad, Randy, Sally, Smitty, Bud and others from La Hacienda, VFW, Sam's, Rio Vista Inn, Kimonos, The Mint, Brando's, Radio Star Karaoke, Doc's Place, Loser's, Troubadours, Metro Café, The Bull Pen, Enkore, and many, many others.

I'd also like to offer a special thanks to Stephanie Jackson, who has researched, edited, rewritten, compiled and labored tirelessly over the past 24 months to be certain that my passion around this book is represented in a cogent and compelling way. Thank you Stephanie!

Finally, thank you to each reader who is willing to look within yourselves and decide to Step up, Inspire and be inspired, Find a Nexus and Go For it! Your world will love you for it!

About the Author

Steve Dragoo is founder and president of Solutions Consulting, Inc. During his 30 plus year career, Steve has worked for major retailers and for two of America's largest food companies. With Solutions Consulting, he has acted as trusted advisor and trainer for some of America's most respected retail supermarket chains and food manufacturers, helping them tell their stories, formulate winning strategies, and continue to win during challenging economic times.

In addition to the book "SING: Business and Life Lessons from the Karaoke Stage", Steve regularly blogs and speaks on the business experience, is frequently interviewed by food-industry publications, and has written "Your Best Store Now" – an e-book offering 99 Ridiculously Easy Tips for Creating a Great Supermarket Experience".

Since the early part of 2001, Dragoo's focus has been to develop and refine a "Customer Experience-Specific" training model. Using multiple resources and field tests, he has created a flexible framework for customized Customer Experience Training that can be adapted and applied to virtually any industry—across a wide spectrum of business situations.

In recognition of his work integrating experience principles into his company's portfolio of offerings, Steve Dragoo was the 2007 recipient of the Experience Management Achievement Award presented by Joe Pine and Jim Gilmore, co-authors of The Experience Economy.

Steve and his wife of 36 years, Nancy live in Nashville Tennessee, near their 3 children and 4 grandchildren.

Steve is available for speaking on a number of topics. His practical, exciting ideas and dynamic presentation style have combined to earn him a highly regarded reputation. His content is relevant and highly-engaging, and audience members will leave with knowledge and tools they can put to use upon their return to the workplace.